WHEN LEADERS
DON'T LEAD

WHEN LEADERS DON'T LEAD

Jill Fandrich, PharmD

ReadersMagnet, LLC

When Leaders Don't Lead; When Coworkers Don't "Co-Work"
Copyright © 2024 by Jill Fandrich, PharmD

Published in the United States of America

Library of Congress Control Number: 2024909434
ISBN   Paperback: 979-8-89091-618-1
ISBN   Hardback: 979-8-89091-619-8
ISBN   eBook: 979-8-89091-620-4

All rights reserved. No part of this publication may be reproduced, stored in a retrieval system or transmitted in any way by any means, electronic, mechanical, photocopy, recording or otherwise without the prior permission of the author except as provided by USA copyright law.

The opinions expressed by the author are not necessarily those of ReadersMagnet, LLC.

ReadersMagnet, LLC
10620 Treena Street, Suite 230 | San Diego, California, 92131 USA
1.619. 354. 2643 | www.readersmagnet.com

Book design copyright © 2024 by ReadersMagnet, LLC. All rights reserved.

Cover design by Jhie Oraiz
Interior design by Dorothy Lee

TABLE OF CONTENTS

Introduction to *When Leaders Don't Lead; When Coworkers Don't "Co-Work"* 7

PART 1 - *When Leaders Don't Lead* 11
Chapter 1: The Incompetent Leader..12
    a. Tolerance..25
    b. Active Listening 32
Chapter 2: The Authoritarian Leader......................................38
    a. Resilience 50
    b. Strategic Thinking 56
Chapter 3: The Narcissistic Leader 64
    a. Gratitude...76
    b. Problem-Solving..80
Chapter 4: The Micromanaging Leader 89
    a. Discernment...99
    b. Effective Communication.................................104
Chapter 5: The Jealous Leader 112
    a. Contentment..118
    b. Delegation..123
Chapter 6: The Corrupt, Manipulative, And Divisive Leader 130
    a. Integrity 135
    b. Time Management...139

PART 2 - *When Coworkers Don't "Co-Work"* 147
Chapter 7: The Disengager..148
    a. Accountability 152
    b. Clear Vision 155

Chapter 8: The Procrastinator 160
    a. Initiative 163
    b. Team Development 167
Chapter 9: The Micromanager 172
    a. Adaptability 175
    b. Conflict Resolution 178
Chapter 10: The Complainer..184
    a. Patience...187
    b. Decisiveness..191
Chapter 11: The Uncommunicator 196
    a. Cooperation 200
    b. Emotional Intelligence 203
Chapter 12: The Resistor..209
    a. Empathy..212
    b. Empowerment 216
Chapter 13: The Disorganizer 222
    a. Orderliness 226
    b. Motivation 229
Chapter 14: The Unproducer 235
    a. Positivity 239
    b. Resourcefulness..242
Chapter 15: The "Entitled" 247
    a. Humility..250
    b. Critical Thinking..254
Chapter 16: Conclusion 260
Journal 265

Introduction for When Leaders Don't Lead

Not all "leaders" have truly earned their titles as "*one who leads*." Many aspiring employees find satisfaction in a job well done. But what if there is no guidance or gratitude acknowledging that your diligent work is transpiring? Have you ever felt singled out or undermined by your leader? Have you ever felt your talents and skills were underutilized? What do you do if your best efforts are unnoticed, unappreciated, or worse yet, "*claimed*" by someone else?

I was speaking at a function regarding a series of my books known as *The Three-Step Process for Personal and Professional Growth*. While many questions were drawn directly from their content, a string of questions began to arise regarding dissatisfaction with leadership. The questions were appropriate, thought-provoking, and…well…concerning!

I listened to question after question and filtered them down to a consistent theme—some "leaders" *aren't actually leading*. The questions were presented in a heartfelt and curious manner, desiring answers to real-life concerns. Why are some leaders not showing appreciation toward their staff? Why are some leaders favoring one employee over another? Why are diligent accomplishments not being acknowledged? Why are some team members being left out of pertinent company meetings? How can these situations be addressed?

I collected valuable information during each of my speaking engagements that followed. I observed leaders, employers, and businesses in general. I read and listened to leadership and success strategies, including my own books and audiobooks, and began to write down the contents of different categories of leaders. I studied and researched effective techniques, questioned influential leaders and diligent employees, and drew from my own leadership experiences as well. This became the premise of the book When Leaders Don't Lead (Part 1.) As my research also revealed issues presented by leaders regarding employees lacking in abilities, I found it vital to include the contents of Part 2 titled When Coworkers Don't "Co-Work."

Part 1 of When Leaders Don't Lead focuses on leadership styles of concern. Each chapter opens with a thought-provoking quote, followed by a description of that particular leader's characteristics. This is informative and validates what you may be experiencing. Every chapter in Part 1 contains a story of an ineffective leader and some of the mistakes made, showing how others were affected by the incompetent behavior. The stories are true and relatable, demonstrating a relevant concern in common description. The chapters then continue by providing ideas, suggestions, and examples of interacting, addressing, and even thriving while working with that type of leader.

Following the related insight, each chapter includes a "*Highlighted Character Quality*" and "*Highlighted Leadership Skill*" to be programmed into your mind and put into practice. Consider the benefits of each listed quality and skill and study ways to develop or improve each one. Read or listen to, understand, and demonstrate each one daily so that by the end of this book, you will have embedded fifteen qualities and fifteen leadership skills into your mind's programming.

The Reflect section at the end of every chapter contains ten points, each with questions or assignments to complete. Do not overlook this section; it is integral to the growing process. Answer, apply, and address all points to get the most benefit from this section. Be mindful in your considerations and critical in your thinking.

Part 2 of *When Leaders* Don't *Lead; When Coworkers* Don't *"Co-Work"* proceeds in a similar format yet focuses on issues that may occur from a *leader's* perspective. As a leader, have you ever felt your employees were giving less than their full potential? Or perhaps not giving much effort at all? Do you have an employee who procrastinates? Or possibly one that tries to take too much control? Nine chapters identify employee behavior issues. Each one begins with a compelling quote, followed by a description and characteristics of the "challenging employee," ways to work and interact with him, and also includes a *"Highlighted Character Quality"* and *"Highlighted Leadership Skill"* for continued personal and professional growth.

Journal on all aspects of the behavior or behaviors of concern. Perhaps focus first on specific behaviors and journal your thoughts and ideas regarding the material. Include the date of entries and the surrounding circumstances. Write down triggers or highlights that stand out, then details that come to mind. Proceed with identifiable characteristics and the techniques you try. Journal about your progress with the strategies you are applying. Take careful notes on what works and what does not. Monitor your progress and update your journal daily or weekly regarding the behavior, obstacles to overcome, and results. Ensure your details are organized enough to be able to refer to the journal for future occurrences. Then, move on to another behavior. Even though you may not currently have a boss or employee acting that way—someday you might! Be proactive and take action now.

In addition, journal daily regarding your progress on character quality and leadership skill training. To get the most out of this book's skill training, work on one quality and one skill per week. Study and apply them daily. As habits can take three or more weeks to develop fully, and this number is different for everyone, you may want to take more time for each one. Once you have mastered one quality and skill, move on to another set to explore, consider, and even master.

This book provides the tools and insight needed to significantly improve your ability to interact with different personality types and perform at your best with favorable and even successful results. It is designed to allow you to jump around to specific behavioral challenges, character qualities, and leadership skills or simply read or listen straight through. For your convenience and quick access, the Table of Contents clearly identifies the location of each one. Whether you read or listen through *When Leaders Don't Lead* chronologically or jump around with a specific category in mind, you will absorb its rich content and learn about various behaviors, ideas, qualities, skills, characteristics, benefits, and strategies to overcome obstacles. Once you have processed the last chapter, go back to the beginning for a refresher! Keep this book handy as a reference for overcoming personality challenges as well as critical leadership skill training. Refer to your journal often for strategies most effective for you in varying situations. Share your best strategies with others. Who do you know that will get the most benefit from this book or your most effective approach?

We spend about a third of our precious day working, including time spent with employees, bosses, colleagues, managers, etc. Make the most of this time and strive for an enjoyable, educational, and even enlightening environment where you can be curious, creative, constructive, and confident and continue to grow personally and professionally in your journey to successfully work effectively with others.

Let the process begin!

PART 1

When Leaders Don't Lead

CHAPTER 1
The Incompetent Leader

Working with an incompetent boss is a test of patience, ingenuity, and resilience. It also reveals the importance of taking initiative, being creative, and leading by example.

—Jill Fandrich

Today is all about Jill.

—Rich N.

Have you ever wondered how your boss worked his way into a leadership position? Did he embody the qualities necessary for that particular job description? Did his leadership skills radiate with ambition and charisma? Was he rightfully chosen over other qualified candidates, perhaps even yourself? Or are his skills "little to be desired," and is it questionable how he got there in the first place? What are the surrounding circumstances? How does he affect you and your performance? How does he affect your employer or company? How about other colleagues? If this is not ideal, what can you do about your situation? What is the best way you can respond?

Incompetent leaders lack the necessary skills and knowledge to lead effectively, resulting in poor decision-making, organizational dysfunction, frustrated and underutilized talent, and sometimes even chaos! If you are reading this book, you may have an issue with your current or even past leader or leaders. You are not alone. While unfortunate, there are many stories about "leaders" who are not leading properly. What are ways this may have happened? How can you amicably work with this type of leader? What can you do to make the best of your situation—or better yet—take steps to improve it?

I was working diligently in my field as a consultant pharmacist, performing tasks and services to the best of my abilities. While I considered my coworkers to be my "equal" colleagues, I have an advanced degree and, therefore, had additional responsibilities, which I embraced with acceptance, discipline, critical thinking, and grace. The relationship with other staff members was engaging, and I was quick to acknowledge each of them and respond to any and all needs I was presented with. I also had an excellent relationship with the DEA and state representatives, among other outside associates who frequented the facilities.

My "boss" was definitely one-of-a-kind. She was clumsy in my hiring, yet I chose to believe she was just busy and displayed a great need for my help, abilities, and varied skill set. I was eager to assist and learn the greatest needs of the facility as well as my boss. I have spent many years in successful leadership roles, including director of many hospital and retail pharmacies. As a matter of fact, I was probably the youngest person in my field to be promoted to a director position within a year of passing my boards. Most of my career had been spent in some form of leadership role. Still, I decided to take a break from this venue and enjoy being a staff employee with an opportunity to work the field as per someone else's guidelines and leadership authority.

After orientation, I experienced one week of one-on-one training infused with countless interruptions. I aggressively took detailed notes and organized them each evening into quick, easy-to-access journal entries. I was grateful I had taken this time at home each evening over the first weekend to make sense of the notes and descriptions of processes, as I was suddenly without any guidance the following week.

The staff was cordial and quick to help, leading me to answers where possible. From this point forward, I may have seen my boss *two* more times that *entire year*! Talk about being thrown into the fire—I was *inflamed* with full responsibility and chose a *"tindered"* spirit. This was most definitely a sink-or-swim situation. As I am not a fan of having my face in the water, I chose to swim! I excelled in my duties and unveiled most of the operation on my own by asking questions, researching where needed, studying policies and procedures, and finding answers, all for the good of the patients and the facility. I grew along with the other staff, and we enjoyed pleasant camaraderie in the spirit of teamwork for a common cause.

I continued this regimen for approximately *four years*, with very minimal contact from my boss. She had obviously trusted my abilities and leadership skills as she failed to participate in the daily operations of any of the clinics I successfully oversaw. The patients were thriving, the staff was working together successfully, and the facilities were growing—until—until my boss suddenly stepped in!

Upper management somehow realized that she hadn't even shown up at my clinics for almost—if not over—a year! There had been virtually no direction or guidance from her during this time. She suddenly appeared with a vengeance, as if she needed to prove something to someone, and the smooth and energized team unity dwindled immediately. She continued with her erratic, emotional, and disorganized rampage for *months* without a glimmer of leadership countenance. She was critical and divisive and resorted to lies, deceit, and unreasonable requests and demands to appear she was "in charge." Feeling a need to raise herself up to look good to her own management team despite not participating in any of my clinics, she had deceived the human resources representative into prefacing her statement with, "*Today is all about Jill...*"

While the words are designed to be complimentary in structure, the intention here was undoubtedly dripping with arrogance and harm. She had a mission to make someone else "look bad" in an attempt to make herself "look good." Unfortunately, her jealousy led her to focus on me in her scope of desperation. These five words—*Today is all about Jill*— echoed through my mind that night as I lay in confusion. My work was exemplary. What was I missing?

A friend of mine often recites the quote, "*I like to go where I'm appreciated, not tolerated.*" Sometimes, he even says, "*... celebrated, not tolerated.*" This also ran through my mind the following days as I considered the incompetence in the management chain. How could my boss, who was able to focus on other things as I completely ran four clinics successfully, become so unhinged? What makes a boss become jealous when supported by her staff? How could a leader ignore four of her own clinics and then take it out on a staff member who ran them so effortlessly without any help and support despite reaching out and sharing results? Shouldn't she be *grateful and appreciative*? Was this where I wanted to share my many gifts and talents? Why did it take so long for *her* boss to realize *she* wasn't leading or managing at all? This facility consisted of management after management being hired based on convenience without inserting leadership training into the mix. The lack of professional skills seeped all the way to the top level of the company.

What makes a good leader? What makes a *great* leader? How would you describe a poor or incompetent leader? How well can you tolerate one? How would you rate the leader described in the previous scenario, absent for four years and then wreathed with illogical and inappropriate control? Have you experienced a similar situation? What were the circumstances? How did you respond? How effective was your response? What did you do well? What areas need improvement? Let's find out more.

This "leader" was the first person to become involved in this facility when no one else was available or desired the particular position. She began to help, and because of her degree, she was able to answer many of the technical questions and concerns. I admit she was very knowledgeable in her licensed field and grew in the concept of "some" of the internal processes and how they were run at this facility. This was a *hire of convenience* and need. What she lacked was *any* semblance or even awareness of leadership abilities.

While her staff grew, she was not instructed by her boss, nor had she taken responsibility for acknowledging the need for or undertaking the development of skills necessary for a leadership role. Her own boss did not even hold her accountable for following company policies regarding employees. In the four-year timeframe, not one annual review or evaluation was executed regarding my service or performance, despite the policies and procedures clearly stating that they were due annually and even quarterly! So, how do you assess an employee's performance *without assessing the employee's performance*? Have you ever worked for a boss who didn't evaluate your performance? Have you known a leader hired based on convenience rather than skill? What is your experience with incompetent leaders? How were you affected? Who else was affected by this situation? What did you do?

Hiring people for positions based on convenience rather than skill is a dangerous practice, especially for leadership roles. Not only is it a disservice to the employees, to say the least, but it can also have negative legal, organizational, and functional implications for the facility.

Dangers of hiring a leadership position due to convenience rather than competence:

1. *Lack of qualifications*: Hiring out of convenience may result in selecting someone not qualified or experienced enough to lead a team or manage a company effectively. This can lead to poor decision-making, disgruntled employees, and ultimately harm the success of the business. For example, while the medical skill set was apparent in the previous scenario, there wasn't even a glimmer of leadership entwined in the boss's personality or abilities. This led her to hire an employee who had a history of felony charges, endangering the reputation of the company and the trust among team members, plus causing a stir with the frequent DEA representatives! While sometimes second chances can be justified, the delicate nature of this particular business did not warrant the colorful background of the hired counterpart, not to mention the company's hiring policy violations. Not only did the boss violate this policy, but her boss did as well. A poor leadership example had been set and imitated. Can you think of a time when a leader lacking qualifications made harmful decisions for the company? Describe the situation.

2. *Negative impact on company culture*: A boss hired for convenience may not align with the company's values and culture, negatively impacting employee morale and motivation. This can result in a disengaged workforce and high turnover rates. It is difficult enough to win over a staff when you are a talented and charismatic leader. However, when a leader is

selected based on convenience rather than skill, it is virtually impossible to corral motivation, let alone respect.

3. *Ineffective leadership*: A boss hired out of convenience may lack the necessary leadership skills, leading to poor communication, low productivity, and a lack of direction for the team. This can result in a decrease in overall performance and hinder the growth of the company. Following the previous scenario, poor communication radiated through the veins of the clinics. Sadly enough, not only was this boss guilty of ineffective leadership and communication, but the "boss apple" did not fall far from the company tree! The ineffective leadership culture permeated the entire company, affecting many different departments, which was evident in the company's disorganization and employee morale.

4. *Conflict and tension*: Hiring a boss for convenience rather than merit can lead to resentment and conflict among employees who may feel the boss does not deserve her position, lead adequately, or treat employees fairly. This can create a toxic work environment and hinder collaboration and teamwork. A boss who lacks the ability to manage and lead her team effectively can lead to low employee morale, dissatisfaction, and disengagement. For example, in the previous story, the boss worked in close proximity to one other employee in the department whom she included in daily plans, invited to all meetings, and kept "in the loop." She excluded everyone else from these pertinent and informative interactions. A skilled leader knows how to treat the staff equally, keep them informed, openly share departmental events, and work cohesively as a team, weaving unity among the staff. An incompetent leader may not have the skills to understand such concepts, essentially *dividing* the team and leading to tension

and discontentment among staff. It is possible, and even likely, that conflicting opinions and responses arise from the discord due to the inadequate and unprofessional way a leader was brought into position in the first place.

5. *Damaged reputation*: A boss who cannot effectively lead and manage her team may damage the company's internal and external reputation. This could have a detrimental effect not only on the boss involved but also on the company as well.

6. *High turnover*: Employees may become frustrated and disheartened working for an incompetent boss, leading to a high turnover rate and increased expenses associated with recruiting and training new employees. Advertising for and hiring new employees is costly in terms of money and time. Training new hires takes time away from other personnel's duties, not to mention the decreased morale of these employees regarding their associates' turnover rate, both from a relationship and increased workload perspective.

7. *Legal and financial risks*: Hiring an unqualified or incompetent boss can lead to legal and financial risks for the company. If the boss makes poor decisions or fails to comply with regulations, the company may face legal repercussions and financial losses. For example, hiring a felon in the medical field monitored by the DEA may lead to legal ramifications. As it turned out, the boss hired by convenience had previously been arrested for criminal charges and possession of drugs, which was known at the time of placement into her position by her boss! In addition, many other company policies were violated, which could lead to negative legal implications from the lack of leadership skills and the absence of necessary training, lending to costly repercussions. Have you ever worked for a company

that suffered legal consequences due to the decisions of an incompetent leader?

Hiring a boss out of convenience, especially one who lacks leadership skills, can have serious negative consequences for a company. Employers should carefully consider a candidate's qualifications and fit before making such an important decision. When a boss lacks pertinent skills, navigating and thriving in such a workplace can be challenging. If you are an employee and the leader's training is not within your scope of purview, what other things could you do to "survive and thrive?"

Ways to work with an ineffective boss:

1. *Lead by example*: Take the initiative to demonstrate strong leadership skills in your own performance and interactions with others. Show your boss and colleagues how effective leadership can positively impact the team and the organization. Make it a daily intention to lead by your positive and inspiring example.

2. *Offer support and guidance*: If appropriate, offer to support your boss by providing guidance and assistance in developing her leadership skills. This could involve sharing articles, books, or leadership resources or offering feedback and support as she works to improve her skills. Consider offering her *The Three-Step Process for Personal and Professional Growth*, found at www.ABookinTime.net. Perhaps slip a copy of each book into a gift bag on an occasion. Suppose your boss is unapproachable or unreceptive to constructive criticism. In that case, you must be charismatic or creative in your supportive attempts, starting with slow and subtle offerings that may not

even be recognizable by your boss as actual guidance. Be persistent and remember to be kind to yourself as you are not only performing your own responsibilities but also reaching out in a selfless act of kindness to positively impact your ineffective leader.

3. *Communicate openly*: If you feel comfortable, consider having a candid and respectful conversation with your boss about her leadership skills. Diplomatically offer specific examples of how her lack of leadership impacts the team and the organization and suggest possible ways to improve. This is a courageous and bold move, so it will take charisma and an offering of kindness as well. Ensure you approach this interaction from a nonjudgmental and objective position in an attempt to avoid putting your boss on a defensive stance.

4. *Seek support from colleagues*: Talk to your colleagues and see if they share the same sentiment about your boss's leadership, ensuring the conversation does *not* take the form of gossip. If they do, consider approaching your boss respectfully as a united front to express your concerns and offer support in developing her leadership skills. How you approach your boss will likely impact the future outcome of the interaction. Put yourself in your boss's shoes and understand being approached regarding this topic by you and your employees or subordinates will require tolerance and openness for growth. If your boss lacks leadership skills, she may not be aware of or in sync with these character qualities.

5. *Document your work*: Keep thorough records of your work and accomplishments, as well as any instances where your boss's ineffective leadership has hindered your ability to perform effectively. A documented record can serve as evidence in future disputes or conflicts with your boss. It can also help you

to recall specific details or conversations that may be important in the future. Documenting your work and interactions can serve as a form of protection against unfair treatment or retaliation from your boss. It can also provide a clear record of your actions and communication, which can be used to defend yourself if necessary.

6. *Focus on your own growth*: If the lack of leadership from your boss is negatively impacting your work and well-being, consider focusing more on your own growth and development. Seek mentorship, training, or coaching opportunities to build your leadership skills and empower yourself to thrive in the workplace. Consider securing a copy of each of the three books in *The Three-Step Process for Personal and Professional Growth* found at www.ABookinTime.net for your benefit! It's important to approach the situation with empathy and a willingness to support your boss in improving her leadership skills yet also take steps to ensure your own well-being and professional growth to benefit your future.

7. *Provide feedback*: Offer constructive feedback to your boss professionally and respectfully, highlighting specific areas for improvement and suggesting potential solutions. Feedback helps identify areas for improvement and insight to make necessary changes to enhance performance. Regular feedback fosters a culture of open communication and collaboration, leading to higher engagement and motivation. *Positive* feedback can boost morale and reinforce desired behaviors, leading to increased job satisfaction and loyalty. *Constructive* feedback provides valuable insights and guidance for personal and professional development. Critically think about which type of feedback will best suit your particular circumstance. Not all bosses will be open to the idea of feedback about themselves.

Consider a "Feedback Sandwich"—positive feedback—constructive feedback—positive feedback. Beginning and ending on a positive note reinforces your good intentions. Feedback can also hold *you* accountable for your own actions and guide you to take ownership of responsibilities. It can even help ensure bosses and teams are aligned with organizational goals and expectations, leading to better overall performance. It is also possible that feedback can stimulate new ideas and creative solutions by encouraging your boss to think critically and approach challenges from different perspectives.

8. *Seek mentorship:* If possible, seek mentorship from a more experienced leader within your organization or even a neutral party outside the company who can guide and support you in navigating the challenges of working with an ineffective boss.

9. *Stay positive and proactive*: Focus on finding solutions and maintaining a positive attitude, even in the face of adversity. This will help you maintain your own motivation and productivity despite the challenges posed by your boss's ineffective leadership. More about developing and maintaining a positive mindset can be found in the book *Elevate Your Mind to Success*.

10. *Take initiative*: Look for opportunities to take on new projects and responsibilities without waiting for your boss to assign them to you. Taking initiative can help you demonstrate your capabilities and contribute to the team's success despite your boss's ineffective leadership. It will also help you redirect your tension more productively and build your skills and confidence.

11. *Respectfully discuss with your boss's boss*: While this is a bold move, if done correctly, it could have a positive outcome for not only you but many other employees and your boss as well.

If upper management is sharp and you know for a fact that they display their own proper leadership skills, approach them privately with your concerns, with the intention of a favorable interaction and outcome. A negative approach will instigate a defensive response and abolish your desired outcome. Analyze your intentions and ensure they are pure and aligned with the right reasons.

12. *Consider transferring to a different position within the company*: While this may not always be possible, if there is an opportunity within the company to transfer to another position with a different boss, weigh out the risks and benefits of taking action in this direction. Discuss with your family, trusted friends, or even a counselor with unbiased intentions, and think logically about the possibility of change. What do you have to gain? What do you have to lose? How would this affect your personal and professional goals? How would it affect your family? Think critically about all of your options.

13. *Seek a new position at a different company*: Sometimes, when all else has failed, it is a logical step to research other employment options. After careful consideration, if you decide it is time to part ways with this company, open your mind to the potentially exciting new opportunities that await. Again, weigh the pros and cons and discuss the idea with trusted confidants. Would you stay in the same field? Is it feasible to drop to part-time and train for a new skill of interest? Explore many different options. Allow your mind to wander to the possibility of a new adventure. Enjoy the journey.

Regarding the incompetent leadership example, I decided to cast caution to the wind and embarked on a new venture. I took a leap of faith and chose to pursue an entirely new career as an author. While it was an unnerving consideration at the time, Rich N. couldn't have been more correct as he said, "*Today is all about Jill.*" These words bring forth precision and continued encouragement as I just finished writing my eighth book, and numbers nine, ten, and eleven are well underway. Once again, I am in a leadership position as my own boss, working from home or wherever I may want to travel to next.

Believe in yourself and your abilities, and embrace the challenges and opportunities of a renewed relationship with your boss or a potentially new career. What have you always wanted to try? What comes easily to you? Stay positive and keep an open mind as you navigate this new path. Trust in your potential to learn and grow in your new role, yet ensure you surround yourself with supportive and encouraging people who believe in you. Remember that it's okay to make mistakes, as they are all part of the learning process. More growth occurs from mistakes than successes. Stay focused and determined, and don't hesitate to ask for help when needed. Be open to new experiences and be willing to step out of your comfort zone. Don't forget to celebrate your successes, no matter how small they are, and keep pushing forward. You have the ability to create the future you want, so go out there and make it happen! Today is all about *YOU*!

Highlighted Character Quality:

Tolerance:

What is tolerance, and how does it fit into leadership? Tolerance is the willingness to accept and respect people and their beliefs, practices, and behaviors, even if they differ from your own. It involves being open-minded, understanding, and accepting of diversity and differences. By no means does it mean you agree with them. Instead, you show respect for the person, not necessarily the content. Tolerance is essential to promoting harmony, understanding, and peaceful acceptance of others or how they interact or present themselves.

Tolerance is necessary for leaders because it allows them to be open-minded and accepting of different perspectives, ideas, and people. Intolerant leaders may struggle to build and maintain a diverse team, make fair and balanced decisions, and effectively communicate with people from different backgrounds. Tolerance also enables leaders to navigate complex and challenging situations with empathy and understanding, ultimately fostering a positive and harmonious work environment. Leaders who demonstrate tolerance can inspire trust and confidence in their team, leading to stronger relationships and improved overall performance.

Tolerance is essential for employees when dealing with ineffective leaders because it allows for understanding and patience in the face of their shortcomings. It means being able to accept and accommodate their limitations without becoming hostile or dismissive. This can be important in maintaining a positive and productive work environment, as well as fostering opportunities for growth and improvement. It also helps to prevent conflict and improve communication, which can be essential in working toward a solution or addressing the issues that arise from poor leadership.

Benefits of tolerance:

1. *Increased empathy:* Tolerance allows you to better understand and appreciate the viewpoints and experiences of others, which can help you develop greater empathy, compassion,

and insight into their perspectives. This can open you up to new appreciation for the input of other contributors.

2. *Broadened perspective*: Being tolerant of different beliefs, cultures, ideas, and work styles can help you develop a more open-minded and unbiased view, which can enrich your life and broaden your perspective. A greater perspective allows for more ideas you may not have considered before and, therefore, many new possible solutions or ways of doing things, perhaps even more efficiently or cost-effectively. If practiced enough, it could become a habit of broadening your perspective and allowing for an expanded mindset and endless possibilities.

3. *Reduced stress*: When you are tolerant of others, you are less likely to feel anger or frustration when faced with differing viewpoints or behaviors. This can lead to reduced stress and a more peaceful mindset. For example, consider how passionate and inflamed most news sources have become. They intend to strike your emotional side to win you over to their perspective. This has led to many stressful events and has aided in people becoming irrational if others do not agree with their viewpoint. Remind yourself it is okay to have different perspectives. Embrace the differences while still respecting the person. More information about disconfirming another viewpoint while affirming the relationship can be learned in the critical thinking book *Who Connects Your Dots?*

4. *Improved communication and relationships*: Tolerance can help you communicate more effectively with a diverse range of people, leading to stronger and more meaningful relationships. Leave negative emotions out and focus on learning and understanding where the other person is coming from and why he holds that perspective. Use critical thinking to gain more understanding while remaining unbiased and without

interruption as you listen with the intention of gaining insight, not focusing on what you want to say next. Once the information is revealed, respond objectively without disregarding his viewpoint. Ask questions if any clarity is needed as you seek to understand.

5. *Enhanced problem-solving skills*: Tolerance can help you approach conflicts and challenges with a more open and flexible mindset. This leads to improved critical thinking, problem-solving skills, and the ability to navigate difficult situations more effectively. Tolerance will also allow you to gain more insight as your mind is more relaxed and open to new thoughts, ideas, and viewpoints.

6. *Personal development*: By embracing tolerance, you can challenge your own biases and assumptions, leading to personal growth and a deeper understanding of yourself and others. Imagine the limitless possibilities of ideas and potential solutions that can evolve with different perspectives.

7. *Social harmony*: Tolerance fosters a more inclusive and harmonious society where people from diverse backgrounds can coexist peacefully. This can lead to a greater sense of community and belonging for everyone. After all, everyone is from the same race—the human race. Embrace the different gifts and talents each person has to offer and notice how much better life can be by highlighting the best in everyone.

8. *Conflict resolution*: Tolerance can help you navigate conflicts and disagreements more constructively, leading to better outcomes and stronger relationships. It can improve resolutions by promoting mutual respect and understanding, allowing you to accept and accommodate differences, and fostering open communication. Tolerance encourages you to listen to

and consider opposing viewpoints, find common ground, and seek peaceful solutions. It also helps to reduce prejudice and discrimination, leading to a more constructive and respectful environment.

It is important to note that tolerance does not mean you must allow others to *force* their perspectives, preferences, or lifestyles upon you. In some current social arenas, policies and regulations are requiring people to conform and even *favor* some preferences or people who "are loud" about *their preferences*. Reread this section for more clarity. Tolerance is essential yet must be utilized appropriately. As a valuable character quality, this is a good time to assess your tolerance level, whether you are a leader or an employee. Everyone is a leader in some respect, such as within a family, circle of friends, or even in another social or community group. Knowing the importance of tolerance, how can you develop or improve upon this valuable quality?

Ways to develop or improve tolerance:

1. *Educate yourself:* Learn about different cultures, beliefs, and perspectives. This can help you understand and appreciate the diversity that exists in your work environment. Also, learn more about the "culture" *within* your workplace and the expectations. Ensure you are well-versed in company policies, goals, and missions, and determine if they align with your values. Perform research regarding tolerance from various online sources. Be intentional and "practice" being tolerant.
2. *Practice empathy:* Put yourself in other people's shoes and try to understand their experiences and feelings. This can help you develop compassion and tolerance toward others. Empathy is

an essential character quality to develop into your mindset. Practice this both personally and professionally. Sometimes, the best way to understand why someone responds the way they do is to understand what they are experiencing. Seek to learn more.

3. *Challenge your own biases*: Be aware of your own prejudices and stereotypes, and make an effort to challenge and overcome any negative ones. This can help you become more open-minded and tolerant. Critically think about the information you receive and the decisions you make. Learn more about critical thinking in *Who Connects Your Dots?* Within this book, you will encounter endless practical applications, allowing you to become fluent at thinking critically, with a higher degree of logical and rational decisions that result.

4. *Learn to communicate effectively*: Develop your communication skills to express your thoughts and feelings in a respectful and understanding manner and actively listen to others. Ensure you think critically before you respond, or better yet, reprogram your mind to automatically respond in a way that is aligned with your values. You can learn how to "Reprogram Your Pre-Program" in *Elevate Your Mind to Success*.

5. *Engage in dialogue*: Have open, respectful conversations with people whose opinions or beliefs differ from yours. This can help you gain new perspectives and increase your tolerance for different viewpoints. By doing this, you are respecting other people and showing them you care about them and what is meaningful to them as well. Ensure you listen carefully and hear what is important to them without interruption. Leaving emotions and opinions aside as you listen to another's perspective is crucial. Overcome any urges to criticize or dismiss their viewpoint or opinion.

6. *Be mindful of your language*: Avoid using derogatory or offensive language toward others. Be conscious of the impact your words can have on others, and strive to communicate in a respectful and encouraging manner.

7. *Practice patience*: Understand that change takes time and effort. Be patient with yourself and others as you work toward becoming more tolerant.

8. *Seek diversity*: Surround yourself with people with different interests, skill sets, backgrounds, and cultures. This can help broaden your understanding and open your mind to new and innovative possibilities. Ask them questions and seek to learn more objectively. Enjoy the process and the learning experience.

9. *Stand up against discrimination*: When you witness genuine discrimination and intolerance, take a stand against it. Discrimination can occur in innumerable ways. This will show respect and allow your leadership abilities to inspire others, creating a more supportive and tolerant environment. Ensure you do this skillfully and respectfully, with the goal of a favorable outcome for everyone. This can be a challenging yet worthwhile endeavor.

10. *Volunteer and give back*: Getting involved in community service and helping others can promote understanding, gratitude, and respect for different perspectives. There is much to be gained by serving others.

11. *Lead by example*: Be a role model for tolerance and acceptance in your own actions and interactions. Good leaders stand out and serve as an inspiration to others. Let others see you are respectful yet will not allow a forced inappropriate action or response.

Highlighted Leadership Skill:

Active Listening:

What is active listening, and how does it fit into leadership? Active listening is a communication technique that involves fully concentrating, seeking understanding, listening, and remembering what is being said. It requires giving the speaker your full attention, showing genuine interest, and providing feedback to demonstrate comprehension. To ensure accurate understanding, active listening also involves asking clarifying questions and summarizing the speaker's points. This technique is important for building strong relationships, resolving conflicts, and improving overall communication.

Active listening is a critical component of effective leadership. When leaders actively listen to their team members, they demonstrate respect, empathy, acceptance, and understanding, which fosters a positive and supportive work environment. Active listening also allows leaders to gain valuable insights and perspectives from their team, which can help in making well-informed decisions, cohesiveness, and solving problems effectively.

Additionally, active listening can help leaders build trust with their team members, showing they are genuinely interested in what their employees have to say. This can increase employee engagement and build cohesiveness, motivation, and satisfaction, contributing to higher productivity and better overall performance.

Benefits of active listening:

1. *Building stronger relationships*: Active listening shows that you value and respect others, which can help strengthen your relationship with them.
2. *Improved understanding*: By truly listening to others, you can gain a deeper understanding of their thoughts, feelings, and needs. This is valuable information.
3. *Conflict resolution*: Active listening can help defuse conflicts by allowing both parties to feel heard and understood.
4. *Enhance problem-solving skills*: By actively listening, you can better understand the root of an issue and work toward finding a solution.
5. *Increased trust and rapport*: When you actively listen to someone, you can build trust and rapport, making communicating and working together easier.
6. *Reduced misunderstandings*: Active listening can help prevent miscommunication and misunderstandings by ensuring that both parties are on the same page.
7. *Personal growth*: Actively listening to others can help you develop empathy, patience, and open-mindedness, which can contribute to personal growth and self-improvement.
8. *Improved communication*: Actively listening can improve your communication skills, making it easier to convey your own thoughts and feelings effectively.

Active listening is a crucial skill for leaders. It enables them to communicate more effectively, build stronger relationships with their team, and ultimately lead their organization to success. How can you improve your active listening skills?

Ways to develop or improve listening actively:

1. *Remove distractions*: Ensure you are in a quiet environment without any distractions, such as your phone, other electronic devices, or other people. Do not allow surrounding elements to distract your attention.
2. *Maintain eye contact*: Show the speaker you are engaged and interested by maintaining eye contact and giving your full focus. Pay attention to your body language in general and ensure you are showing interest.
3. *Avoid interrupting*: Let the speaker finish his thoughts before responding. Interrupting can make the speaker feel unheard, unimportant, or irrelevant and may cause him to lose his train of thought.
4. *Show empathy*: Try to understand the speaker's perspective and empathize with his interests and experiences.
5. *Ask clarifying questions*: If you are unclear about something the speaker said, ask for clarification. This shows that you are actively trying to understand his thoughts and perspectives.
6. *Reflect on what you heard*: Summarize the speaker's words to show that you actively listened and understood the message. Consider what he wants you to know and why.
7. *Practice mindfulness*: Be present in the moment and focus on the speaker's words without letting your mind wander. Take in the context and the intent of the content. Be intentional and make yourself aware of the process of listening actively.
8. *Be open-minded*: Approach the conversation with an open mind and be willing to listen to different perspectives. Set all preconceived notions aside and remain objective.

9. *Practice active listening*: Practice active listening in everyday conversations to improve your skills and become a better listener.

10. *Seek feedback*: Ask the speaker for feedback on how well you listened to and understood the message. This will help you identify areas for improvement. Work continually to improve your ability to listen actively.

Working for a boss who lacks leadership abilities is difficult and challenging, to say the least. While you cannot control the situation, there are some things you can try that may positively impact your working environment. Take some time to review the suggestions presented in this chapter. Critically think about your specific situation and try the ideas that seem most appropriate to you. Review the *Highlighted Character Quality* and *Highlighted Leadership Skill* in this chapter and apply them both personally and professionally. Build a supportive and positive team culture, focusing on collaboration and cooperation with other coworkers to overcome the leader's deficiencies. If necessary, escalate the issue to higher management or HR for intervention and support in addressing the ineffective leadership. Chances are, if you have identified this issue, other team members will be dealing with the same problems as well. Be the change you want to see.

 Reflect:

1. Have you ever worked for an incompetent or ineffective boss? How did you deal with this type of behavior? What were the results? What did you do correctly?

2. What changes will you make as a result of this chapter? What is your desired outcome?

3. Where does the ineffective behavior stem from? Is it solely with your immediate boss, or is there an issue with the company's management in general? What will you do if the issue is only with your boss? What will you do if it is company-wide?

4. What are some dangers of an incompetent leader? What can you do when faced with this situation? What can you add to the list provided in the chapter?

5. What do you know about tolerance? How can tolerance be used effectively in leadership? Describe a time when you lacked tolerance. Describe a time when you were tolerant despite challenges. Compare and contrast each example. What do you notice?

6. Find ways to program tolerance into your "preprogram." More information about how to "Reprogram Your Pre-Program" is found in *Elevate Your Mind to Success, Success Is Ele-MENTAL*, and at www.ABookinTime.net.

7. Describe what it means to actively listen to someone. How is it used effectively as a leader? How can it be used effectively as an employee?

8. Rate your current ability to listen actively. What are you doing correctly? How can you improve?

9. What are some benefits of actively listening? How can this be applied to a situation involving an incompetent or ineffective leader?
10. Research more about tolerance and active listening and practice these valuable skills daily.

CHAPTER 2
The Authoritarian Leader

Bad leaders believe in the power of their position, while great leaders believe in the power of their people.

—Jill Fandrich

Courage is not the absence of fear but the triumph over it. The brave man is not he who does not feel afraid but he who conquers that fear.

—Nelson Mandela

An authoritarian leader is a boss who exercises strict control over his employees, often using fear, intimidation, and domination to maintain power and authority. He typically has a top-down management style, making decisions unilaterally without input from team members. An authoritarian boss may be demanding, critical, and quick to reprimand or punish employees for perceived mistakes or shortcomings. He prioritizes obedience and compliance, often disregarding the well-being and input of employees. This type of boss can create a toxic work environment characterized by high levels of stress, low morale, and a lack of autonomy for the employees.

A friend of mine shared a similar story regarding hiring for a management position by convenience. He worked within the same company but in a different department under other "leadership." I will call this friend Phil. As I witnessed, Phil was a diligent, ethical, professional, and hard-working employee. He valued his job and position within the company and treated other staff and patients with the utmost respect. Phil also had a "boss of convenience." Ironically, Phil was initially offered the leadership position but declined. A man of equal "ranking" as Phil, whom I will call Dom, was then asked to take the position.

Human Resources didn't take the time to advertise the position and open it up to the community for potentially qualified talent. Instead, they cut corners and promoted internally in an attempt to save money and fill the opening immediately. Dom was quick to blame others and slow to take responsibility for his own actions, if at all. He made decisions to his benefit rather than regarding how others were affected. Like my boss, Dom had no leadership skills or formal management training, yet he accepted the offer and filled the position effective immediately.

Dom led by emotion and "fire-fighting"—he extinguished one fire after another without a plan or direction. He quickly developed an authoritarian leadership style, using intimidation as a "tactic" to gain control over employees and force them into compliance since he didn't know how to lead effectively. Authoritarian leaders rule with an iron fist, using fear and intimidation to control their staff and suppress dissent. Not having the essential skills led Dom to frustration and emotional outbursts, negatively impacting the entire staff. This was a no-win scenario with an unskilled person thrown into the position with neither leadership nor position-specific training. He manipulated and disincentivized his staff with intimidation and a punitive approach, further alienating and dispersing the team's unity.

Have you ever worked for a boss who lacked leadership skills and led with negative authority, using intimidation and emotion?

How about manipulation or even punitive responses? What was it like working for someone with this temperament? How did you respond? How did other staff members respond? Describe the team dynamics. What was the turnover rate of employees? How productive was the staff as a whole? How can you be the voice of change under these conditions?

Ways to work with an authoritarian boss:

1. *Understand his perspective:* Attempt to understand where your boss is coming from, his expectations, and what triggers his intimidating behavior. This will help you approach him with empathy and understanding.

2. *Establish clear goals:* Clearly defined goals will help alleviate some unnecessary confusion. Seek to understand his goals for you and the company in general. If possible, meet with him individually and physically write out a list of expectations. This will allow you always to be aware of them and your boss to see your determination and intent to understand. Ensure you have a copy of your job description and follow it completely. Do not leave any room for unnecessary criticism.

3. *Be prepared:* Before approaching your boss, ensure you are well-prepared and have all the necessary information and resources at hand. This will show your boss that you are serious and capable. Collect as much information as possible and allow yourself to be well-informed in each situation. Respect his time and be brief and punctual in your approach.

4. *Communicate openly:* Be honest and direct in your communication with your boss. Avoid beating around the bush and address any issues or concerns directly. Be decisive and

assertive, ensure your approach is open, and refrain from being critical, defensive, or accusatory. Also, be aware of your body language so you don't send any unintentional messages. Ask for any clarity you need during this time.

5. *Be respectful*: Approach your boss with respect and professionalism. Use a calm and composed tone of voice and maintain eye contact. Show concern and allow him to see your interest in his success as well as the success of the company. Display that you are a team player and are committed to collaborating with other employees. Be tolerant in your responses and practice patience.

6. *Set boundaries*: Establish clear boundaries with your boss to ensure that you are treated with respect. Be assertive in utilizing your rights and standing up for yourself when necessary. Research and even practice setting boundaries aligned with your values. While setting boundaries may be a reasonable and logical task, following through on them may be more challenging. Ensure this occurs as well.

7. *Seek feedback*: Ask for feedback on your performance and how you can improve. This shows your boss that you are open to learning and growing. Positively respond to the feedback in the sense of your desire to continually learn and improve your skills and performance. Extract information from each interaction you have with your boss and adjust where necessary. Every interaction is an opportunity to learn something new.

8. *Build a relationship*: Try to build a positive and professional relationship with your boss. Find common ground, look for opportunities to collaborate, and show your value to the team. Make it known that you can be trusted and will show respect for everyone on the team. Be cautious that this type of person

doesn't try to build you as an ally for his advantage while opposing other peers. Stay true to yourself, your boss, the company, and your peers.

9. *Stay calm and composed*: When dealing with an intimidating boss, keep your emotions in check. Respond in a calm and composed manner, even if he is aggressive or confrontational. Remain objective and set emotion aside, knowing the problem is with the authoritarian boss without leadership training. Use critical thinking to reason each situation out.

10. *Stay confident*: Believe in yourself and your abilities. Confidence can go a long way in dealing with an intimidating boss. Continue to work on your own personal and professional growth. Take time to boost your confidence, as working for an authoritarian boss can damage your self-esteem. Do not allow this damage to happen. Stay on top of your physical and mental health.

11. *Focus on results*: Ensure you consistently deliver high-quality work and meet deadlines. Showing your boss that you are a reliable and valuable team member can help alleviate some of the punitive behavior. Stay one or more steps ahead at all times.

12. *Focus on a positive mindset*: Focus on positive self-talk, affirmations, or declarations to build your self-esteem and resilience. Transform any negative energy into positive energy. Learn to "Reprogram Your Pre-Program" as instructed and defined in *Elevate Your Mind to Success*.

13. *Document interactions*: Keep a record of any intimidating or inappropriate behavior from your boss. This can be useful if you need to address the issue with HR or higher management.

You could also keep records of your successes to document your value. It is a shame to have to do this, but it could be a win-win activity—you are reaffirmed of your own value, and it serves as a record for future use to your boss or company, exemplifying your effectiveness in the company. It could also be used as a source to refine your resume for future use.

14. *Seek support*: If you are struggling with your boss, seek support from a mentor, colleague, friend, or the HR department. They may be able to provide guidance and support in managing the situation. They could also give you the boost you need to know you are not alone. Sometimes, that may be all that is needed.

15. *Turn in your resignation*: There may come a point when you decide it is not worth your time and effort to stay under these conditions. If you have exhausted other possible solutions and you are still unsettled, begin your search for a new beginning. You could choose to follow suit and keep the peace at work while spicing up your resume. Consider all your options, including your potential to try something you have never tried before. Maybe you are being led in another direction, and an amazing new future awaits you. Be open to new possibilities. Be sure to follow company policies and procedures when resigning. What other ideas can you think of to effectively work with an authoritarian leader?

Working for an intimidating and emotional boss can be very challenging. It is important to understand his behavior is outside the realm of your control. As long as you are not doing anything to cause the negative reactions intentionally, you must release any guilt you may place upon yourself and recognize any attempt he may make to cause you to feel guilty or pressured. Beware that you don't conform to the unfavorable circumstances. While it is beneficial to be a team player and try to keep the peace, establish and know your boundaries and do not let them be crossed to appease your boss.

Have you ever allowed yourself to feel guilty about your boss's negativity? Has his intimidation ever caused you to make decisions you wouldn't normally make? Have you ever allowed your boss's behavior to carry on into your home and personal life? How did this affect you? How did it affect your family? How did this affect your work performance? What things can you try to do to release the guilt or self-pressure you feel due to your boss's actions?

Ways to release guilt or self-pressure when dealing with an intimidating boss:

1. *Understand your feelings*: Recognize and acknowledge your feelings of guilt or pressure and their source. It's important to understand that the guilt or pressure you feel may not necessarily be justified. A boss who is acting inappropriately is the one with the problem. Unfortunately, this spills over onto the employees, forcing you to make judgment calls. Challenge the thoughts you are thinking. Has your boss made requests or demands that are unrealistic? Is there any truth or validity to them? Reveal your thoughts to yourself and challenge them at the core. Critically thinking about the intimidation can reveal insight into your boss. What do you discover?

2. *Reduce stress*: Practice deep breathing and mindfulness to help calm your nerves and reduce anxiety. What do you currently do to reduce stress in your life? What hobbies do you enjoy? Do you pray through your circumstances? Does meditation help clear your mind? What else helps to reduce stress?

3. *Communicate with your boss*: If your boss's behavior contributes to your feelings of guilt or self-pressure, consider having an open and honest conversation with him. Respectfully express your concerns and discuss how his behavior is impacting you. Due to the intimidating nature of the boss, this may be a challenging approach to take. Find a way to make it less threatening. Take another employee with you, communicate in the form of an email, or bring it up in a highly populated area. Whatever brings you a sense of confidence will aid in instigating this communication. Just remember to be respectful and professional in your approach. Document your interaction.

4. *Set boundaries*: Establish clear boundaries with your boss to protect yourself from feeling guilty unnecessarily. This may involve setting limits on the amount of work you take on or asserting yourself when you feel unfairly criticized. Align boundaries with your values and know where you stand. Establishing boundaries can build confidence, as you will not leave circumstances to chance and will have a guideline for what you will and will not accept.

5. *Stay focused*: Focus on the task at hand rather than worrying about the intimidating boss. Challenge your thoughts and release any fear that creeps in. Have your goals set, and do not sway from them. Stay in control of yourself and your "mission" or responsibilities. Focus on performing your task to the best of your ability.

6. *Seek support*: Talk to a trusted colleague, friend, or mentor about feeling pressured. Getting an outside perspective can help you gain clarity and support. Even the act of talking out loud as you share your concerns with others works a different part of your brain as you hear the issues verbalized. Your mind

explores other areas of potential resolution, providing more options of possibility and a greater probability of success.

7. *Practice self-compassion*: Remember that it's okay to make mistakes or feel unsettled when working with an intimidating boss and that you are doing your best. Self-care and self-compassion counteract negative feelings of anxiety and self-pressure. Be kind to yourself as you continue to grow and look for solutions. When your mind is not boggled down with mental clutter, it is more open to discovering new possibilities.

8. *Seek professional help*: If your unsettled feelings are persistent and impacting your mental health, consider seeking support from a therapist or counselor. They can help you work through them and develop healthy coping strategies. It is important to ensure you don't let guilt or unwarranted pressure get the best of you. Address the issues before they expand.

9. *Focus on your strengths*: Remind yourself of your skills, accomplishments, and contributions. Building self-confidence and self-worth can help you combat negative feelings. Your boss's response and reactions are beyond your control, but you do have control over yourself and your personal and professional growth. Continue to expand your mind and improve your skills and knowledge. Transform negative energy into positive energy and use it to your benefit. *The Three-Step Process for Personal and Professional Growth* is found at www.ABookinTime.net.

10. *Focus on staying healthy*: Remember to make your health a priority. Establish a nutritious diet, try a routine intermittent fasting schedule, exercise regularly, get adequate sleep, stay well hydrated, and ensure you are healthy mentally as well. You think the best when your system is healthy and well-

maintained. Boost your body's immunity naturally and avoid chemicals your body sees as foreign. A healthy body supports a healthy mind.

11. *Practice self-awareness*: Take a step back and analyze your thoughts and feelings. Are they based on reality, or do your perceptions exaggerate them? Understanding the source of any negative pressure can help you manage it more effectively. Are you pressuring yourself in any way because of your boss? Is your boss directly or indirectly pressuring you? How is this affecting your performance? Challenge your thoughts and reveal the truth of the situation.

12. *Set realistic expectations*: Understand that you cannot control your boss's behavior, but you can control your own reactions. Set realistic expectations for yourself and focus on what you can control.

Working for an intimidating boss is a challenging situation. Previously, we identified some options for approaching this type of person. While we hope he will learn and grow from your skillful examples of professionalism and respect, this is not always, or maybe even rarely, the case. Understanding your inability to control him and releasing any tendencies to try is important. You can only control yourself—your reactions, responses, thoughts, perceptions, and especially your own growth and development. Sometimes, it may be difficult to let go of attempting to control someone other than yourself. You may want to see this person excel in their leadership and positively affect the company. Yet, the decision must be their own. Focus on your own professionalism and lead by example.

Ways to release the need to "try to" control your boss's bad behavior:

1. *Identify the root cause:* Reflect on why you may feel the need to want to control the situation or person. Understanding the underlying emotions and fears can help you address them effectively.
2. *Focus on what you can control:* Instead of trying to change your boss's behavior, focus on how you can respond in a way that is in *your* best interest. This might involve setting boundaries, communicating assertively, or seeking support from others.
3. *Practice acceptance:* Accept that you cannot control your boss's behavior and that trying to do so will only lead to frustration and stress. Instead, practice accepting the situation and focusing on how you can manage your reactions and emotions. Build up your own skills, both practically and professionally. Learn from your boss's ineffectiveness and apply this insight to your own development. Be determined to use this information and turn a negative situation into a positive opportunity.
4. *Identify your triggers:* Reflect on what specifically about your boss's behavior triggers your desire for control. Understanding your triggers can help you develop strategies for managing your reactions and letting go of the need to try to control him.
5. *Seek support:* Talk to a trusted colleague, mentor, or professional about your experiences. Sometimes, just expressing your frustrations and concerns can help you release the need to seek to control his behavior and actions.
6. *Focus on self-care:* Engage in activities that help you relax and reduce stress, such as exercise, prayer, meditation, or hobbies.

Taking care of yourself can help you feel more resilient and better able to cope with challenging situations.

7. *Set realistic expectations:* Understand that you may not be able to change your boss's behavior, but you can control how you respond to it. Set realistic expectations for yourself and focus on how you can manage the situation effectively.

8. *Develop self-awareness*: Pay attention to your thoughts and behaviors, and recognize when you are trying to control a situation. Take a step back and consider alternative perspectives and approaches.

9. *Embrace flexibility*: Allow room for spontaneity and change in your life. Being open to new possibilities and adapting to unexpected outcomes can help you let go of the need for control.

Remember that releasing the need to try to control your boss's inappropriate behavior is a process that takes time and practice. Be patient with yourself and seek support when needed. Practice mindfulness by learning to be present in the moment and observe your thoughts and emotions without judgment. This can help you recognize your possible controlling tendencies and consciously let go. Even if your intentions are pure, the responsibility is not yours. Accept that there are things in life that are beyond your control. Embrace the uncertainty and trust that things will unfold as they are meant to. Replace this focus with a renewed focus on your own advancement and growth. This is something you can control.

When interacting with an intimidating boss, remaining calm and composed is important. Take deep breaths and try to relax your body to avoid showing signs of nervousness. Show respect to your boss by using polite language and maintaining a professional demeanor. This may be difficult as you will unlikely see the same respect extended back to you. Avoid interrupting him and listen attentively to what he has to say. It's important to project confidence when interacting with an intimidating boss. Stand tall, make eye contact, and speak with a clear and assertive voice. Before meeting with your boss, make sure to prepare for the interaction. Anticipate any questions or concerns he may have and come prepared with solutions or answers.

Be honest and transparent in your communication with your boss. If you have any concerns or issues, address them respectfully and constructively. Ask him for feedback on your work and performance. This shows you are open to constructive criticism and willing to improve. Even while your boss is intimidating, it's important always to maintain a professional attitude. Avoid getting defensive or argumentative, and keep the conversation focused on work-related matters. Look for opportunities to build rapport with your boss by finding common interests or engaging in casual conversations when appropriate. This can help to humanize your boss and make interactions less intimidating.

Highlighted Character Quality:

Resilience:

What is resilience, and how does it fit into leadership? Resilience is the ability to adapt and recover from difficult or challenging situations. It involves the capacity to bounce back from adversity, cope with stress, and maintain a sense of well-being and optimism in the face of adversity. Resilience is a valuable trait that helps you navigate life's ups and downs and build the strength to overcome obstacles.

Resilience is a key trait for effective leadership, enabling leaders to navigate challenges, setbacks, and adversity with grace and determination. Resilient leaders are able to remain calm and composed in the face of adversity, inspire and motivate their teams to overcome obstacles, and bounce back from failures with a positive attitude. They are able to adapt to changing circumstances, learn from their experiences, and continue to move forward toward their goals. Resilience allows leaders to maintain their focus, drive, and effectiveness in leading others, even in the most difficult circumstances. Resilience can also be crucial when dealing with ineffective people.

Benefits of resilience:

1. *Positive mindset*: Resilience can help you maintain a positive mindset and focus on finding solutions rather than dwelling on others' shortcomings or challenging situations.
2. *Better mental health*: By being resilient, you are better equipped to handle stress, adversity, and challenges, leading to improved mental health and a reduced risk of developing mental health disorders.
3. *Improved physical health*: Research has shown that if you are resilient, you are more likely to engage in healthy behaviors, such as exercising regularly and eating nutritiously, which can lead to improved physical health and a reduced risk of chronic diseases. This leads to an overall improved quality of life.
4. *Adaptability*: Resilience allows you to adapt to changing situations and find ways to work through challenges, ensuring that your work and productivity are not significantly impacted.

You can also adapt to different people with diverse perspectives and enjoy the differences you encounter.

5. *Problem-solving*: Resilience can help you develop problem-solving skills, enabling you to find creative and innovative solutions to work around the challenges posed by ineffective people and difficult situations.

6. *Emotional regulation*: You can better regulate your emotions and maintain composure in difficult situations, enabling you to handle interactions more effectively. Resilience involves managing and regulating emotions in difficult situations. As you build resilience, you can develop greater "emotional insight," leading to improved self-awareness, empathy, and interpersonal skills.

7. *Learning from experiences*: Resilience allows you to learn from your experiences and use them as opportunities for personal growth and self-improvement. By reflecting on your resilience in challenging situations, you can gain valuable insights and develop a greater understanding of yourself and your abilities, leading to more self-confidence.

8. *Building confidence*: When you demonstrate resilience in the face of adversity, you can develop a sense of self-efficacy and confidence in your ability to handle difficult situations. This confidence can foster personal growth and empower you to take on new challenges and pursue your goals.

9. *Overcoming obstacles*: Rather than become immobilized or wallow in distress, resilience enables you to bounce back from setbacks and challenges. This allows you to continue moving forward and learning from your experiences, which can lead to personal growth as you develop problem-solving skills, adaptability, and perseverance.

10. *Self-motivation*: Resilience can help you stay motivated and focused on your own goals and performance despite the challenges you face. Draw from this passion and determination and continue in a positive direction.

11. *Greater success*: Being resilient means being more likely to persevere in the face of challenges and setbacks, leading to greater success in your personal and professional lives. Resilience is closely linked to a growth mindset, which involves believing in your ability to grow and improve through effort and perseverance. Embracing a growth mindset can lead to personal growth as you become more open to learning, taking on new challenges, and seeking out opportunities for self-improvement.

12. *Better relationships:* You are better able to navigate conflicts and setbacks in relationships with resilience, leading to stronger and more fulfilling connections with others. You are also more adaptable and open to different perspectives, showing tolerance and acceptance in your interactions.

13. *Greater sense of purpose*: With resilience, you are better able to find meaning and purpose in your life, leading to a greater sense of fulfillment and satisfaction. You are content with your choices.

14. *Improved coping skills*: Being resilient you are better able to cope with and recover from traumatic events, leading to a reduced risk of developing conditions such as anxiety, post-traumatic stress disorder (PTSD), and other mental health issues. You are also able to handle smaller setbacks with grace and even admiration.

15. *Seeking support*: With resilience, you are more likely to seek support from colleagues, mentors, HR, or trusted friends when

dealing with adversity, ensuring you have the resources and guidance needed to navigate the situation effectively.

As resilience is a valuable character quality, this is a good time to assess your resilience level, whether you are a leader or an employee. Everyone is a leader in some respect, such as within a family, circle of friends, or even in another social or community group. Knowing the importance of resilience, how can you develop or improve upon this valuable quality?

Ways to develop or improve resilience:

1. *Pre-program a positive mindset*: Focus on the things you can control and find ways to reframe negative situations in a more positive light. Learn how to "Reprogram Your Pre-Program" as described in *Elevate Your Mind to Success*. Discover the source of negativity, replace it with positive thoughts, and declutter your mind. Find out more at www.ABookinTime.net.

2. *Build a strong support system*: Surround yourself with people who uplift and support you during difficult times. Align yourself with like-minded people and build strong and supportive relationships. Do not underestimate the importance of a reliable support system.

3. *Develop problem-solving skills*: Approach challenges with a solution-oriented mindset and actively seek ways to overcome obstacles. Be resourceful and creative. Chapter Three will discuss how to develop your problem-solving skills further.

4. *Practice self-care*: Be good to yourself by caring for the health of your body systems. Take time for activities that remove harmful substances from your body in a healthy way. Make healthy living a priority—detoxify your body from impurities via

"detox baths," sweating out toxins, and "clean eating." Find out more about detoxification at www.ABookinTime.net.

5. *Set realistic goals*: Break down larger goals into smaller, achievable steps to build confidence and momentum. Enjoy the small wins with each accomplishment. As your confidence increases, let the size of your goals increase as well.

6. *Embrace change*: Learn to enclasp new situations and explore the possibilities that come with change. Be flexible and face them with positive energy and even an excitement for opportunities for growth and new experiences. "Launch" yourself into new challenges with confidence and eager curiosity.

7. *Reflect on past experiences*: Review past challenges, consider what helped you overcome them, and apply those lessons to current situations. Learn from your experience, both the good and the bad. You grow the most during challenging times. Extract the benefits from your personal experiences.

8. *Practice gratitude*: Focus on what you are grateful for and find ways to express appreciation for the positive aspects of your life. Make this a daily practice to recognize what you are thankful for.

9. *Practice mindfulness and relaxation techniques*: To help manage stress and build inner strength, engage in activities such as meditation, deep breathing exercises, praying, participating in your favorite hobby, or even Pilates. Allow these activities to bring you joy and relaxation.

10. *Take care of your physical health*: Regular exercise, a balanced diet, proper hydration, and adequate sleep can help improve your overall well-being and increase your ability to handle stress. Focus on building your natural immunity.

11. *Foster adaptability*: Situations often don't unfold as you would like or expect them to. Be open and even learn to expect new experiences. Flexibility and the ability to adapt to new circumstances can help you bounce back from adversity. Learn to be prepared and to "expect the unexpected." Have backup plans and take the opportunity in stride. This will also help you reduce stress.

12. *Seek professional help if needed*: If you are struggling with resilience, consider speaking with a therapist, counselor, or another person skilled in resilience who can provide guidance and support. Resilience is a valuable and necessary character quality. Who do you know that embodies this quality? Spend more time with this person.

13. *Practice resilience-building activities*: Engage in activities that promote resilience, such as mindfulness meditation, journaling, reading and educating yourself in various areas, or seeking out new experiences. Find opportunities that are resilient-specific and practice daily.

Highlighted Leadership Skill:

Strategic Thinking:

What is strategic thinking, and how does it fit into leadership? Strategic thinking is the ability to analyze complex situations, identify patterns and trends, and develop long-term plans and goals to achieve desired outcomes. It involves anticipating potential challenges and opportunities, making informed decisions, and adapting to changing circumstances. Strategic thinking also involves considering various factors such as resources, capabilities, competition, and market dynamics to develop effective strategies for success. It requires creativity, critical thinking, and a broad perspective to anticipate and plan for potential obstacles and opportunities.

Strategic thinking is a crucial component of effective leadership. It involves analyzing complex situations, anticipating future trends, and developing long-term plans to achieve organizational goals. Leaders with strategic thinking skills are able to make informed decisions, prioritize tasks, and allocate resources effectively. They are also adept at identifying opportunities and risks by forward-thinking, having a proactive mindset, and adapting their plans in response to changing circumstances.

Strategic thinking enables leaders to see the big picture and align their actions with an organization's vision and mission. They are able to communicate a clear direction to their team members and inspire them to work toward common objectives. Additionally, leaders who demonstrate strategic thinking are better equipped to navigate uncertainty and lead their company through periods of change and transformation.

Strategic thinking is essential for leaders to create and sustain a competitive advantage for their business and to drive long-term success. It allows them to be proactive, innovative, and adaptable in their approach to leadership.

Benefits of strategic thinking:

1. *Better decision-making*: Strategic thinking helps you evaluate different options and anticipate potential outcomes, leading to more informed and effective decision-making. You see a broader scope of potential ideas or solutions to choose from and are more confident in your final decisions.

2. *Improved problem-solving*: This enables you to identify and address underlying issues and challenges, leading to more sustainable solutions. You draw from more resources and innovation to solve problems more effectively and efficiently.

3. *Enhanced adaptability*: Strategic thinking allows for a proactive approach to change and uncertainty, enabling you to better navigate and respond to evolving circumstances. You are flexible and more tolerant in your approach.

4. *Increased innovation*: Strategic thinking fosters a mindset open to new ideas and creative solutions, leading to a culture of innovation and continuous improvement.

5. *Competitive advantage*: Strategic thinking allows you to anticipate and respond to market trends, customer needs, and competitive threats, positioning you for long-term success. You are prepared for challenges and have an "edge" over the competition.

6. *Better resource allocation*: It helps to prioritize and allocate resources effectively, ensuring that time, money, and talent are utilized in the most impactful way. You develop "resource insight."

7. *Long-term focus*: It encourages focusing on long-term goals and objectives rather than short-term gains, which leads to more sustainable and enduring success.

8. *Stronger leadership*: Strategic thinking fosters a leadership style that is visionary, collaborative, and able to inspire and guide you toward a shared vision and successful outcome.

9. *Increased organizational alignment*: Strategic thinking encourages open communication and collaboration among team members. It enables you and your associates to work

toward common goals and objectives, fostering greater alignment and unity within an organization.

10. *Personal growth and development*: Strategic thinking encourages you to develop critical thinking, problem-solving, and decision-making skills, leading to personal and professional growth.

Strategic thinking is an important skill for both employees and leaders to embrace. It allows you to make informed decisions and contribute to the company's overall success. By utilizing strategic thinking skills, you can analyze complex problems, identify the root causes, and develop innovative solutions to address them. Strategic thinking helps you make well-informed decisions by considering the long-term impact and weighing the pros and cons of various options. With strategic thinking skills, you can develop and implement plans that align with long-term objectives and goals. It also allows you to anticipate potential challenges and changes in the business environment, enabling you to adapt and adjust your approach accordingly. Strategic thinkers can effectively collaborate with colleagues, share ideas, and contribute to the development of strategic initiatives that benefit a company as a whole, contributing to success by being proactive, forward-thinking, and focused on creating value for the company.

Ways to develop or improve strategic thinking:

1. *Develop a long-term perspective*: Strategic thinking involves looking beyond immediate problems and considering the long-term implications of decisions. Developing a long-term perspective can help you anticipate future challenges and

opportunities. Think about the future and consider the "big picture."

2. *Stay informed*: Keep yourself updated with the latest industry trends, market developments, and competitor activities. This will help you make informed strategic decisions and identify new growth opportunities. Read as much as you can. Exposing yourself to a variety of ideas, perspectives, and theories can help you develop a more nuanced and well-rounded understanding of the world, which is crucial for strategic thinking.

3. *Foster creativity*: Encourage creativity and innovation within your team to generate new ideas and perspectives. This can help you develop more effective and unique strategic solutions. Be open to new perspectives and consider them objectively.

4. *Analyze and synthesize information*: Practice analyzing complex data and synthesizing information from different sources to gain a deeper understanding of the situation. This will help you make more informed and effective strategic decisions.

5. *Embrace uncertainty*: Develop the ability to navigate uncertainty and ambiguity. Be willing to step out of your comfort zone and take calculated risks based on careful analysis and evaluation. Strategic thinking often involves making decisions in uncertain environments, so being comfortable with ambiguity can help you make better decisions.

6. *Set clear goals*: Having clear and specific goals can help you focus your thinking and make more strategic decisions that align with your long-term objectives. Ensure your goals are in writing and update them daily, weekly, or at least monthly.

7. *Collaborate with others*: Seek input and feedback from diverse perspectives within your organization or from trusted peers.

Collaborating with others can help you gain new insights and identify blind spots in your strategic thinking.

8. *Develop critical thinking skills*: Enhance your critical thinking skills by questioning assumptions, evaluating evidence, and considering alternative viewpoints. Do extensive research and ask unbiased questions. This can help you make more objective and rational strategic decisions. You can learn and even program critical thinking skills into your mind by reading or listening to *Who Connects Your Dots?* or *Students: Who Connects Your Dots?*

9. *Learn from past experiences*: Reflect on past strategic decisions and their outcomes to learn from successes and failures. This can help you avoid repeating mistakes and improve your strategic thinking skills. Learn from your own mistakes as well as those of others.

10. *Develop a strategic mindset*: Cultivating a mindset focused on long-term goals, big-picture thinking, and proactive planning can help you improve your strategic thinking abilities.

11. *Practice scenario planning*: Develop the ability to anticipate different possible scenarios and their potential impact on your organization. Scenario planning can help you prepare for different future outcomes and make more resilient strategic decisions.

12. *Seek feedback*: Ask for feedback from colleagues, mentors, or trusted advisors to gain insights into your strategic thinking abilities and identify areas for improvement. Feedback can help you refine your approach and enhance your strategic thinking skills.

13. *Continuously learn and adapt*: The world is constantly changing, and the best strategic thinkers adapt and evolve their thinking

in response to new information and developments. Continuous learning and openness to new ideas are essential for improving strategic thinking.

14. *Improve your decision-making skills*: Consider the potential outcomes of different choices and make decisions based on thoroughly evaluating the available information. Use critical thinking in your decision-making.

Strategic thinking is essential in various aspects of life, including business, leadership, decision-making, problem-solving, and personal development. It allows you to set long-term goals, anticipate challenges, and adapt to changing circumstances effectively. By thinking strategically, you can make informed decisions, allocate resources efficiently, and stay ahead of the competition. Ultimately, strategic thinking helps achieve sustainable success, growth, and innovation in both personal and professional endeavors.

 Reflect:

1. Have you ever worked for an authoritarian boss? How did you deal with this type of behavior? Was he intimidating as well? What were the results? What did you do correctly?

2. What changes will you make as a result of this chapter? What is your desired outcome?

3. Where does the authoritarian behavior stem from? Is it solely with your immediate boss, or is there an issue with the company's management in general? What will you do if the issue is only with your boss? What will you do if it is company-wide?

4. What are some dangers of an authoritarian leader? What can you do when faced with this situation? What can you add to the list provided in this chapter?

5. What do you know about resilience? How can resilience be used effectively in leadership? Describe a time when you lacked resilience. Describe a time when you portrayed resilience despite challenges. Compare and contrast each example. What do you notice?

6. Find ways to program resilience into your "preprogram." More information about how to "Reprogram Your Pre-Program" is found *in Elevate Your Mind to Success, Success Is Ele-MENTAL*, and at www.ABookinTime.net.

7. Describe strategic thinking. How is this used effectively as a leader? How can it be used effectively as an employee?

8. Rate your current ability to think strategically. What are you doing correctly? How can you improve?

9. What are some benefits of thinking strategically? How can this be applied to a situation involving an authoritarian boss?

10. Research more about resilience and strategic thinking and practice these valuable skills daily.

CHAPTER 3
The Narcissistic Leader

A narcissistic leader is like a mirror that only reflects his own image, leaving no room for the growth and development of others.

—Jill Fandrich

A narcissistic leader may shine brightly for a moment, but his ego will eventually overshadow his ability to inspire and lead others.

—Jill Fandrich

Narcissistic leaders are self-centered people only concerned with their own power and success, often at the expense of others. It is most often under this style of leadership that you feel unappreciated and unnoticed. It could even be to the extent that you feel used, as you are performing at your best, yet the boss takes credit for your work. Have you ever worked for a boss who took credit for your work? How about one who failed to show any kind of appreciation or acknowledgment for your work? How did it make you feel? What was the surrounding scenario? Who was affected by his actions? How did you respond? Are there other employees who experienced similar treatment?

What causes a leader to dismiss the hard work and participation of the team members? How can they possibly accept all your hard work without recognizing your efforts and sacrifice? How often is your work overlooked? How often are you overlooked? Is there anyone else whom the boss doesn't acknowledge? Is the boss focused on his own image and success, or is it a matter of lacking skills to understand the importance of supporting and appreciating staff?

Jamie had been working for a company for over two years and felt "burned out." She was accustomed to hard work, pulling her own weight and generally giving beyond that. Jamie had begun in the fall when she first noticed an opening for her skill set at a company located conveniently to her home. Orientation was brief, and the staff was sparse. She could tell they were in desperate need of more help. Still, she accepted the position and worked diligently, paying attention to detail and even providing foresight to big presentations, resulting in the company landing some new and prestigious accounts.

Jamie had brought new perspectives, innovation, and fresh creativity to the table, yet she found herself unappreciated and even overlooked for a promotion to someone with much less experience. While she didn't resent this other employee, as he did what was logical and accepted the position, she lost motivation. She found herself turning sour over the lack of acknowledgment for her astounding and sacrificial accomplishments, leading to the apparent growth of the company and accolades for the boss. Why was her boss reluctant to acknowledge Jamie and show gratitude toward her? Why didn't Jamie receive the credit she clearly deserved?

Jamie's boss continued to be known for his narcissistic tendencies. He would constantly brag about his accomplishments, belittle his employees, and demand constant praise and attention. He would spend valuable time talking about himself in meetings, rarely taking time to listen to Jamie or other team members' ideas or concerns. He expected everyone to cater to his every whim and would throw tantrums if things didn't go his way. Despite his arrogance and self-centered behavior, Jamie's boss managed to climb the corporate ladder thanks to his manipulative tactics, taking credit for his employee's work, and ability to charm those in higher positions. Jamie, however, lived in constant fear of his wrath and struggled to meet his unrealistic expectations. As time passed, the boss's behavior began to take its toll on Jamie and the team. Morale was low, turnover rates were high, and productivity suffered. Slowly but surely, the once successful department started to crumble under the weight of their narcissistic boss's ego. Jamie finally saw through his façade, the unchecked narcissism, and realized the damage he had caused. She chose to be free from the toxic grip of the narcissistic boss who had once ruled over her.

Reasons why a boss may not show appreciation:

1. He may be too busy or preoccupied with other responsibilities to express appreciation.
2. He may believe showing appreciation for doing a good job is unnecessary.
3. He may have a different leadership style and does not prioritize expressing appreciation to his employees.
4. He may not be aware of the impact of showing appreciation on employee morale and motivation.
5. He may have high expectations and believe employees should perform well without needing constant praise.
6. He may not have been taught or trained on the importance of showing appreciation to employees.

7. He may feel uncomfortable or awkward expressing appreciation and prefers to focus on the task at hand.
8. He may be dealing with personal or professional challenges that prevent him from showing appreciation.
9. He may not value the employees' contributions or take them for granted.
10. He may have a negative or critical mindset that makes it difficult for him to express appreciation.
11. He may be jealous of the employee's talents and choose not to highlight or even acknowledge them.
12. He may have a toxic or other narcissistic personality and lack empathy.

Right or wrong, there are numerous reasons why a "leader" may not be "leading." Can you identify your boss's reason? Why is he unable to show appreciation for your contributions? Is it from the list mentioned, or do you know another reason? Or maybe there are many reasons. Praise can go a long way in a world where budgets are tight and costs are consistently being cut. Employees are generally content and encouraged with "praises for raises" when an actual raise is not currently possible. But what happens when there is no raise *and* there is no praise? Several negative consequences may occur.

Potential consequences when employees are NOT appreciated:

1. *Decreased morale*: Employees' motivation and morale can decrease when they feel unappreciated. This can lead to a lack of enthusiasm and engagement in their work, resulting in reduced productivity and performance.

2. *Increased turnover*: Employees who do not feel valued by their boss may seek other employment opportunities. This can lead to increased turnover and the loss of valuable talent within the organization. Quite often, as one employee leaves due to unappreciation and lack of motivation, a domino effect will likely occur, and other unsatisfied employees will follow suit.

3. *Poor work environment*: Unappreciated employees may disengage, creating a negative work environment. This can impact the organization's overall culture and lead to decreased collaboration and teamwork. It may actually be worse than the domino effect of employee turnover. In this case, the disgruntled employee doesn't leave but rather stays around to "poison the water cooler."

4. *Lack of loyalty*: Employees who do not feel appreciated may become less loyal to the organization. They may not be as invested in the company's success and may be more likely to leave when presented with other opportunities. Worse yet, they may engage in other outside work endeavors during company time.

5. *Health issues*: The stress and dissatisfaction of feeling unappreciated can lead to health issues for employees, including increased levels of anxiety, depression, and burnout, as Jamie was experiencing.

When your boss does not appreciate you, it can have a detrimental impact on your well-being, performance, and the overall success of the organization. It is essential for leaders to recognize and acknowledge their employees' contributions in order to create a positive and productive work environment.

What if that person is you? Are you currently in an unappreciated situation? How have you tried to gain appreciation from your boss?

How about other coworkers? Where does the unappreciation stem from? Is it with one person or more than one? What is your desired outcome? What do you like about your current job and responsibilities? Is it worth finding a solution so you can maintain your position but with a newfound energy and well-deserved appreciation?

Dealing with a narcissist is a very tricky and intentional endeavor. This personality type has probably developed in their childhood and will most likely never change. There are some things you could try to open the doors of communication and let it be known that you would like to be acknowledged and appreciated for your skilled work and contributions.

Ways to relay your concerns:

1. Schedule a one-on-one meeting with your boss to discuss your concerns and express your desire to be appreciated for your contributions. Be professional yet friendly and non-threatening in your approach, and ensure you do not put them on the defensive. If they appear defensive, you may need to reschedule the meeting until they are open to hearing what you want to share more objectively.
2. Use specific examples of your work and accomplishments to demonstrate your value to the team and the organization. Be factual and brief, yet thorough, so your point will be clear and memorable.
3. Share how being appreciated for your efforts will increase your motivation and productivity. Focus on what may positively impact the company and the boss as well. Show him how he would benefit from your feeling appreciated and needed in

the company and on his team. As you are aware, a narcissist wants to know what's in it for him. Use this knowledge to your advantage and seek a win-win scenario. Stand up for your needs, but do it carefully in a way that benefits both parties. This step of bravery could further spill out to other employees and build an environment of healthy, productive, and happy camaraderie. Remember to set boundaries in your interactions and expectations.

4. Ask for feedback on your performance and how to improve while expressing your need for recognition and validation. This also gives the boss a sense of control, which would massage his ego. It puts him in the driver's seat while letting him know you care about your performance and how he and his department will be affected by it. From a legal perspective, it is good to document your request for feedback as a "thermometer" for how you are doing, showing your concern and desire to improve. When interacting with a complex personality such as a narcissist, you may want to watch your back and get some things in writing. You never know when it may come in handy.

5. Emphasize the importance of a positive and supportive work environment for your overall well-being and job satisfaction. As a narcissist wants to know how he will gain, allow him to see the benefits of a healthy and positive staff. Describe how an appreciated staff will be more pleasant to work with while being more open to creativity and new perspectives.

6. Suggest implementing regular performance reviews or recognition programs to acknowledge and reward employees for their hard work. Suggest ideas of how to show appreciation. Perhaps he is unaware of not only the need to show gratitude but also *how* to show it. Discuss with the staff beforehand and get their input on how they would like to feel appreciated.

Present the best ideas to the boss with enthusiasm for his participation. You will also exemplify leadership skills by identifying problems and bringing forth possible solutions. This is an admirable quality—find a need and meet it. In this case, identify a need and present potential solutions to resolve it.

7. Seek out opportunities to showcase your skills and expertise in front of your boss and colleagues to demonstrate your value to the organization. Sometimes, the best way to learn is by visualization or example. Be the example you want your boss to be. Recruit other staff members to join in and highlight their value. Ensure all this activity is done from a positive mindset to grow favorably rather than out of spite or other negative responses. Make it fun, and enjoy the process. Show your boss the benefits of positive energy and appreciated employees.

8. If your boss is open to feedback, express your desire for more positive reinforcement and acknowledgment of your contributions. Be blunt and come right out and say it. Again, say it from a positive mindset and a win-win position. After all, the goal of every position is to work together for the common good of the company. You could even suggest a trial run of some ideas. Chances are great that the process would continue due to the positive responses coming from the staff.

9. Show appreciation to your boss. If your boss makes any effort to respond to the ideas presented, show appreciation for his willingness to try. It is not easy to admit you are wrong or acknowledge a fault. Not showing appreciation is most definitely a leadership fault. Be kind in your interactions and give him credit where credit is due. Also, even outside of an attempt, if your boss does not acknowledge any of the ideas mentioned, show your boss appreciation in any act of leadership he presents, as hard as it may initially be. Thank

him for any guidance, suggestions, orders, instructions, etc. "Kill him with kindness," so to speak. Let him witness firsthand what kindness and appreciation are like. Remember, this personality type may not have experienced much kindness in his upbringing. It may be foreign to him and cause him to be uncomfortable changing his ways. Yet, continue to show respect and display your own character qualities in all of your interactions.

10. If you have exhausted all other ideas and efforts, you may need to resign and find a position where you are appreciated and can grow and flourish. Be professional and give your full notice and the company time to find a replacement. If they request an exit interview, take the opportunity to share what happened, what you attempted to do, and the outcome. Keep it factual and objective, leaving emotion and bias out. Then, prepare for an amazing new beginning somewhere else, doing something else you get to choose. As my friend Will says, *"I would rather go where I'm celebrated, not tolerated."*

For the most part, there are similar steps to be taken if you have a boss who isn't necessarily a narcissist yet just doesn't get the concept of showing gratitude. Dealing with this type of boss can be frustrating, but handling the situation professionally is important. Communication is always the key. Schedule a one-on-one meeting to discuss your concerns. Be respectful and express how his lack of appreciation makes you feel. Provide specific examples of when you felt unappreciated and how it impacted your morale. Ask for feedback on your performance and how you can improve. This can open up a dialogue and show your boss you are open to constructive criticism.

If your boss consistently disregards your efforts, setting boundaries and managing your expectations may be necessary. Focus on your work ethic and personal satisfaction rather than seeking validation from your boss. Lead by example. Continue to perform at a high level and demonstrate your value to the organization. Show that you are motivated by personal discipline and a strong work ethic rather than external validation.

If the lack of appreciation continues, seek support from HR or a trusted mentor within the organization. They can provide guidance on how to address the issue and advocate for your recognition. Remember that if you feel this way, others may also feel this. Your actions may positively impact several people, including your boss and peers.

If you have a good relationship with one of your peers, you could even discuss using each other as a type of "accountability partner" but in the sense of an "appreciation partner." Encourage and support each other and openly show gratitude for a job well done or tremendous effort for a project. In one respect, you will receive the appreciation needed to drive motivation and allow for a more sustainable work environment. On the other hand, the boss may learn from the example you and your peer have set. Be professional and diplomatic in your actions. Most importantly, be genuine. Experiment and see if this is something that will work in your setting.

Consider all of your options. If the situation does not improve and it becomes clear that your boss does not value your contributions, you may need to consider seeking opportunities elsewhere. Working in an environment where your efforts are appreciated and recognized is important.

Working with a narcissist can present several challenges. They often lack empathy, have a sense of entitlement, and can be highly manipulative. Their constant need for attention and validation can create a toxic work environment, and their difficulty in accepting feedback or criticism can lead to strained relationships with colleagues. Additionally, their tendency to take credit for the work of others and their inability to collaborate effectively can hinder team productivity. Blame and unaccountability are two of their common attributes. Overall, working with a narcissist can be emotionally draining and can hinder professional growth and success.

Ways to work with a narcissistic boss:

1. *Set boundaries*: Clearly communicate your limits and expectations to your boss and be firm in enforcing them.
2. *Document everything*: Keep a record of all interactions, including emails and conversations, with your boss to protect yourself in case of any disputes and also to serve as a record of all of your accomplishments. With a narcissistic tendency to blame and dodge accountability, you want to be well-protected with documentation.
3. *Seek support:* Connect with colleagues or a mentor who can provide guidance and support in dealing with a narcissistic boss. You may even want to keep them closely involved to "back you" if you ever need to corroborate a story.
4. *Focus on your work*: Stay focused on your tasks and responsibilities, and avoid getting entangled in your boss's ego-driven behavior.
5. *Communicate effectively*: Use assertive communication techniques to express your concerns and needs to your boss

in a professional manner. Always be clear, decisive, diplomatic, and specific when communicating with him.

6. *Manage your emotions*: Practice self-care and seek help from a therapist or counselor to manage the stress and emotional impact of working with a narcissistic boss. Be kind to yourself, and do not accept any unwarranted guilt.

7. *Seek alternative solutions*: Consider transferring to a different department or seeking new opportunities if the situation becomes unbearable. Narcissists are difficult to deal with on any level. Release any feelings of guilt if this is the path you choose to take.

8. *Confront the behavior*: If appropriate, confront your boss about his behavior and its impact on the team and work environment. Be confident yet diplomatic in your approach.

9. *Develop a support network*: Build relationships with other colleagues and superiors who can provide support and advocate for you in challenging situations.

10. *Consider leaving*: If the situation becomes unmanageable and affects your well-being, consider finding a new job with a healthier work environment. Working in an environment where you can grow, blossom, and expand your horizons unyieldingly is important.

Working with a narcissistic boss can be extremely challenging due to their self-centered and manipulative behavior. They may be highly critical and unwilling to listen to feedback, making it difficult to communicate effectively with them. Their need for constant validation and attention can create a toxic work environment, and their lack of empathy can lead to unfair treatment of employees. Additionally, their tendency to take credit for others' work and blame others for their mistakes can lead to frustration and demotivation among the team. Working with a narcissistic boss can be emotionally draining and detrimental to your professional growth and well-being.

Consider the previously mentioned ideas and suggestions on how to interact and communicate your needs and desires. Depending on whether your boss has a narcissistic personality type or just lacks some necessary leadership skills, success in the quest for appreciation may be determined. Study and apply the following highlighted character quality and leadership skill for your continual journey for personal and professional growth.

Highlighted Character Quality:

Gratitude:

What is gratitude, and how does it fit into leadership? Gratitude is the quality of being thankful and showing appreciation for the good things in life. It involves recognizing and acknowledging the positive aspects of life and other people and feeling thankful toward them or your Creator. Practicing gratitude has many positive effects on mental and emotional well-being.

Gratitude is essential to effective leadership as it helps build trust, rapport, and positive relationships with team members. Leaders who express gratitude for their team members' hard work, dedication, and contributions create a supportive and motivating work environment, which can lead to increased morale, job satisfaction, and productivity among team members.

Furthermore, expressing gratitude can also help leaders recognize the efforts and achievements of their team, which can lead to improved employee engagement and retention. When team members feel appreciated and valued, they are more likely to be loyal and committed to the organization and its goals.

Gratitude can help leaders foster a culture of positivity and appreciation within their teams, leading to better teamwork, collaboration, and overall performance. By showing gratitude, leaders can inspire and motivate their team members to continue delivering high-quality work and strive for excellence. It is a powerful tool in effective leadership, creating a positive and supportive work environment and fostering a culture of appreciation and teamwork.

Benefits of gratitude:

1. *It fosters a positive mindset*: When you practice gratitude, you focus on the good things in your life, which can help shift your mindset from a negative to a positive one. This positive outlook can help you approach challenges with resilience and optimism, leading to personal growth. More about positive mind transformation is found in *Elevate Your Mind to Success*.

2. *It promotes self-awareness*: Practicing gratitude encourages you to reflect on what you are thankful for, which can increase self-awareness and help you understand what truly matters to you. This self-reflection can lead to personal growth as you gain a better understanding of your values, goals, and priorities.

3. *Better physical health*: When you show gratitude, you tend to engage in healthier behaviors, such as regular exercise, adequate sleep, and seeking medical help when necessary. This leads to improved physical health and an overall improved quality of life.

4. *It enhances emotional well-being*: Gratitude has been linked to lower levels of stress, anxiety, and depression. By

cultivating gratitude, you can improve your emotional well-being, experience more relaxation, and develop the resilience needed to navigate life's challenges, which can contribute to personal growth.

5. *It strengthens relationships*: Expressing gratitude toward others can strengthen your relationships and build a supportive network. This can provide opportunities for personal growth through collaboration, learning, healthy interactions, deeper connections, and mutual support.

6. *Enhanced self-esteem*: Gratitude helps you appreciate your own accomplishments and value your contributions, leading to a greater sense of self-worth and confidence.

7. *Better sleep*: Practicing gratitude has been shown to relax your mind and improve the quality and duration of sleep, leading to better overall health and well-being.

8. *It encourages a growth mindset*: Gratitude can help you develop a growth mindset where you view challenges as opportunities for learning and development. This mindset can lead to personal, professional, and spiritual growth as you embrace new experiences and strive to improve yourself.

9. *Increased empathy and compassion*: Gratitude encourages a focus on the needs and feelings of others, leading to more compassionate and empathetic behavior.

10. *Increased resilience*: When you are grateful, you are better able to cope with stress and adversity. You can focus on the positive aspects of your life and find meaning and purpose in difficult situations. This gives you increased motivation and resilience to successfully work through adversity and face it head-on.

Now that you know the importance of gratitude from both a personal and professional aspect, how can you program more gratitude into your mind?

Ways to develop or improve gratitude:

1. *Daily gratitude practice*: Start your day by listing three things you are grateful for. Show appreciation for these things in a way of your own choosing. This can help to shift your focus from what you lack to what you have. Make this a habit to do each day.
2. *Gratitude journal*: Keep a gratitude journal and write down things you are grateful for each day. This can help reinforce a gratitude mindset and serve as a documented record of the multitude of things you have to be thankful for. Read through previously written entries often.
3. *Mindful appreciation*: Practice being present in the moment and noticing the small things you are grateful for, such as a beautiful sunset or a kind gesture from a friend. You do not have to look far to find things to appreciate. Find beauty in your surroundings.
4. *Express your thanks*: Make an effort to express your gratitude to others. This can be through a simple thank you note or a heartfelt conversation. Even something as simple as a kind wave while in traffic. Make this effort a daily habit.
5. *Shift your perspective*: When faced with challenges, reframe them as opportunities for growth and learning. This can help to cultivate a mindset of gratitude even in difficult times.
6. *Surround yourself with positivity*: Spend time with people who have a positive outlook and who themselves practice gratitude.

Their energy can be contagious and help reinforce your own mindset of gratitude.

7. *Practice self-care*: Taking care of yourself and prioritizing your well-being can help you feel more grateful for your health, opportunities, and resources available to you.

8. *Volunteer:* Giving back to others and contributing to your community can foster a sense of gratitude. Volunteering your time and skills to help those in need can help you appreciate what you have and feel more grateful.

9. *Reflect on challenging experiences*: Sometimes, difficult experiences can help you appreciate the good things in life. Reflecting on past challenges and how you have overcome them can help you develop a sense of gratitude for your resilience and strength.

Highlighted Leadership Skill:

Problem-Solving:

What is problem-solving, and how does it fit into leadership? Problem-solving is the process of finding solutions to difficult or complex issues. It involves identifying the problem, analyzing the situation, brainstorming potential solutions, evaluating them, and implementing the best course of action. It often requires critical thinking, creativity, and perseverance to overcome obstacles and reach a resolution. Effective problem-solving skills are valuable in various aspects of life, including personal, academic, and professional settings.

Problem-solving is a crucial skill for effective leadership. Leaders often encounter complex and challenging situations requiring them to identify and analyze problems, develop potential solutions, and make decisions to address the issues at hand. There are many ways in which problem-solving is used in leadership situations.

Benefits of problem-solving:

1. *Better communication skills:* Problem-solving often involves working with others and communicating effectively to find a solution. This can lead to improved communication skills and the ability to work well in a team.
2. *Identifying and defining problems:* Effective leaders are able to identify and define the root causes of problems within their teams or organizations. They use critical thinking and data analysis to accurately diagnose issues and understand their implications. As you work toward solving problems, more revelation about the issue can occur, leading to more effective solutions.
3. *Personal growth:* Successfully solving problems can lead to personal growth and development as you learn from your experiences and become more resilient and resourceful.
4. *Generating and evaluating solutions:* Leaders use problem-solving skills to brainstorm and evaluate potential solutions to address identified problems. They consider various options, weigh pros and cons, and assess the potential impact on the organization.
5. *Increased creativity:* Problem-solving often requires thinking outside the box and developing innovative solutions. This can lead to increased creativity and the ability to think in new and different ways, which can be used to effectively resolve future concerns.

6. *Increased productivity*: Problem-solving can lead to more efficient and effective ways of doing things, which can ultimately increase productivity.

7. *Making reasoned decisions*: Leaders must make informed decisions based on their problem-solving process. They consider all relevant information, consult with others as needed, and ultimately choose the best course of action to resolve the problem at hand.

8. *Enhanced adaptability*: Problem-solving requires flexibility and the ability to adapt to new situations, which can lead to improved adaptability in all areas of life.

9. *Implementing solutions*: Once a decision has been made, leaders must take action to implement the chosen solution. They use their problem-solving skills to develop and execute a plan, allocate resources effectively, and monitor progress to ensure that the solution is successful.

10. *Enhanced resilience*: Successfully solving problems can build resilience and the confidence to tackle future challenges.

11. *Greater self-confidence*: Successfully solving problems can boost self-confidence and self-esteem, as it demonstrates the ability to overcome obstacles and achieve goals.

12. *Learning from failure*: Problem-solving in leadership also involves learning from mistakes and failures. Effective leaders use setbacks as opportunities to reflect, adapt, and improve their problem-solving approach to future challenges.

13. *Improved interpersonal relationships*: Problem-solving often involves working with others and can lead to better relationships and teamwork skills.

14. *Better stress management*: Developing problem-solving skills can improve stress management, as you will feel more equipped to handle challenges and setbacks.

Problem-solving is a key component of effective leadership, as leaders must be able to navigate uncertainty and complexity, make tough decisions, and drive positive change within their organizations. It is an essential skill in personal growth as well. Working toward developing or improving your ability to solve problems is important.

Ways to develop or improve problem-solving abilities:

1. *Practice critical thinking*: Engage in activities that require you to analyze information, find the truthfulness in it, make decisions, and solve problems. This can include puzzles, brain teasers, and logic games. Ask many questions and seek unbiased information. Critical thinking is analyzing and evaluating information, arguments, and evidence objectively and logically. It involves actively questioning and examining assumptions, beliefs, and biases and using reasoning and evidence to create well-informed and reasoned judgments. Critical thinking also involves the ability to think creatively, consider multiple perspectives, and make connections between different ideas and concepts. It is a key skill for problem-solving, decision-making, and effective communication. More information on critical thinking can be found in the book *Who Connects Your Dots?* and at www.ABookinTime.net.
2. *Break problems down*: When faced with a complex issue, break it down into smaller, more manageable parts. This can make identifying the root cause and finding a solution easier. Dividing

it into smaller parts helps clarify the different components and makes it easier to understand and less overwhelming, allowing for better focus on each aspect. This leads to a more thorough analysis and understanding. Addressing smaller parts allows for more targeted problem-solving and the ability to identify specific solutions for each component. This can facilitate collaboration as different team members can take ownership of specific parts and work together to address the overall issue. Breaking a complex problem into smaller parts can also increase confidence in tackling the issue as it becomes more manageable and approachable.

3. *Learn from experience*: Reflect on past problem-solving experiences and consider what strategies worked well and what could be improved. Use this knowledge to tailor your approach to future problems. Ask yourself critical thinking questions about the experience. Remain unbiased as you ask and seek to collect objective insight, allowing your mind to expand with creative and possibly innovative ideas and perspectives.

4. *Use visualization techniques*: Picture the problem and potential solutions in your mind to help clarify your thinking and develop innovative ideas. Ensure you have already decluttered your mind so it is open and free from heavy, dense, or negative thinking.

5. *Develop a growth mindset*: Embrace challenges and view failures as opportunities for learning and growth. Make daily learning an automatic entry on your goals list.

6. *Seek out challenges*: Embrace opportunities to tackle complex problems, whether at work, in personal projects, or in everyday life. The more you practice problem-solving, the better you will

become at it. Enjoy the process and consider the challenges as opportunities for growth.

7. *Collaborate with others*: Working on problem-solving tasks with colleagues, friends, or family members can expose you to different perspectives and approaches, helping you expand your problem-solving skills. Diversity will help you see things from different points of view, providing more opportunities for effective resolutions.

8. *Stay open-minded*: Be willing to consider various potential solutions and be open to trying new approaches. Avoid getting stuck in a rut by always approaching problems with a flexible mindset. Choosing an open-minded approach increases the likelihood of finding the best method of solving the issue. You will have new alternatives and strategies you would have never had if you proceeded with a narrow outlook.

9. *Develop your creativity*: Creative thinking can lead to innovative problem-solving solutions. Engage in activities that stimulate your imagination, such as art, writing, or brainstorming exercises. Constantly challenge your creative side and seek inspiration from different sources. Try new things and be open to new possibilities. Embrace failures and use them to your advantage to explore more creativity.

10. *Seek feedback*: Ask for feedback from others on your problem-solving approach. This can help you identify blind spots and areas for improvement. Insight from others who see things from a different perspective will shine a new light you may not have seen before. Take advantage of the opportunity to learn from the gifts, talents, and perspectives of other people.

11. *Learn new skills*: Acquiring new knowledge and skills can provide you with additional tools for solving problems. This can

include learning about decision-making, conflict resolution, and communication techniques. More knowledge will contribute to new thoughts and ideas, adding potential new ways to solve old problems.

12. *Stay resilient*: Problem-solving can be challenging, and not every attempt will be successful. Cultivate resilience and perseverance to keep trying, even when faced with setbacks. Staying resilient when problem-solving is essential because it allows you to bounce back from setbacks and continue to pursue solutions. Resilience helps you maintain a positive attitude and persist in facing challenges, leading to more effective problem-solving. Additionally, staying resilient can help you learn from failures, adapt to new information, and ultimately find creative and successful solutions to problems. Overall, resilience is essential for overcoming obstacles and achieving success in problem-solving.

13. *Stay organized*: Use tools such as mind maps, lists, or diagrams to visually represent and organize information related to the problem at hand.

Problem-solving is crucial in both personal and professional life. It helps you overcome challenges, make informed decisions, and achieve desired goals. It enhances critical thinking skills, fosters creativity, and promotes innovative solutions. Effective problem-solving leads to improved communication, collaboration, and overall productivity. It also helps you adapt to change, learn from your experiences, and continuously grow and develop. Problem-solving is a fundamental skill essential for success in various aspects of life.

 Reflect:

1. Have you ever worked for a narcissistic boss? How did you deal with this type of behavior? What were the results? What did you do correctly?

2. What changes will you make as a result of this chapter? What is your desired outcome?

3. Where does the narcissistic behavior stem from? Is it solely with your immediate boss, or is there an issue with the company's management in general? What will you do if the issue is only with your boss? What will you do if it is company-wide?

4. What are some dangers of a narcissistic leader? What can you do when faced with this situation? What can you add to the list provided in this chapter?

5. What do you know about gratitude? How can gratitude be used effectively in leadership? Describe a time when you lacked gratitude or appreciation. Describe a time when you openly showed appreciation despite challenges. Compare and contrast each example. What do you notice?

6. Find ways to program gratitude into your "preprogram." More information about how to "Reprogram Your Pre-Program" is found in *Elevate Your Mind to Success, Success Is Ele-MENTAL*, and at www.ABookinTime.net.

7. Describe problem-solving. How is this used effectively as a leader? How can it be used effectively as an employee?

8. Rate your current ability to problem solve. What are you doing correctly? How can you improve?

9. What are some benefits of effective problem-solving? How can this be applied to a situation involving an unappreciative or narcissistic boss?

10. Research more about gratitude and effective problem-solving and practice these valuable skills daily.

CHAPTER 4
The Micromanaging Leader

Micromanaging leaders are like puppeteers who control every movement of their puppets, stifling the creativity and potential of those they seek to control.

—Jill Fandrich

A micromanaging boss is like a lurking shadow—it may follow you everywhere but can never dim your light.

—Jill Fandrich

A micromanaging leader controls and interferes with her subordinates' work, stifling creativity and productivity. She closely oversees and controls every aspect of her team's work, often to the point of excessive and unnecessary detail. She is known for constantly checking in on her employees, scrutinizing their every move, and giving frequent, unsolicited feedback on even the smallest tasks. This type of leader tends to be overly controlling, lacks trust in her team, and can stifle creativity and productivity. She may also struggle to delegate tasks and empower her employees, leading to a lack of autonomy and motivation within the team. A micromanaging leader can create a tense and stressful work environment and hinder the potential growth of her team and, therefore, the company in general.

Have you ever worked for a micromanager? How were you affected? Did it just affect your professional life, or was your personal life affected as well? How were your other team members affected? What was the impact on the company? How did you respond to the microscope method of management? How did your peers respond? Were the responses effective?

Returning to the story from chapter one, the previously aloof boss of four years underwent a transformation when pressed by upper management. She transitioned from never being around and offering no input to micromanaging every detail of work and undermining employees with every chance in an evident display to lift herself and her self-esteem up. She resorted to lies and deception in an attempt to justify her absenteeism and to glorify herself. It became known how well I led the team and how successful the clinics were. The morale was high, and we worked together, supporting each other as a unified team. By her choice, the boss had not been a part of this, and in her case, although I had been respectful and supportive toward her despite her absentee-leadership, her insecurity led her to begin to micromanage what "wasn't broken" instantly.

She began to constantly check in on employees and question their every move, dictated every detail of how tasks were to be completed without allowing for any input or autonomy from employees, and monitored work closely and frequently without trusting the employees to do their jobs independently. She also became overly critical of minor mistakes yet didn't provide constructive feedback or support. She insisted on being copied on every email and included in every decision, no matter how small. Tasks were assigned haphazardly, causing confusion and inefficiency. In addition, by not allowing employees to take ownership of their work or make decisions on their own and undermining their authority, she created a work environment filled with stress, anxiety, and a lack of trust among team members.

The clinics went from smooth, well-run, pleasant camaraderie to tense, clumsy, and undesirable conditions. It is astounding how *one person* can negatively impact an entire department and even a clinic in such a short period of time. It was very unfortunate that the "one person" happened to be *the boss*.

So, why might someone micromanage in the first place?

Reasons a leader might micromanage:

1. *Lack of trust*: Without constant oversight, the leader may not trust her employees to complete tasks to the desired standard.
2. *Perfectionism*: The boss may have high standards and want to ensure that every detail is executed exactly as she envisions.
3. *Control issues*: The manager may feel the need to maintain control over every aspect of the work to feel secure and in charge.
4. *Fear of failure*: The leader may be afraid that things will go wrong if she doesn't micromanage and will be held responsible.
5. *Insecurity*: The leader may feel insecure in her own abilities and feel the need to overly involve herself in every task to feel competent.
6. *Lack of delegation skills*: The boss may not know how to delegate tasks and responsibilities effectively, which may lead her to micromanage instead.
7. *Pressure from higher-ups*: The leader may be pressured by her superiors to closely monitor and control her team's work.

8. *Jealousy*: The leader may be jealous of her employees and seek to "take their thunder" to make herself look good or temporarily feel better about herself.

9. *Incompetence*: Not having the proper leadership skills can itself be a reason the boss micromanages, attempting to find a method that works while showing her boss she is actively doing something.

If you are working diligently and are performing your best, it's time to understand that the issue is NOT with you. It is with your boss. She is the one with the problem. Often, if you can find the source of the problem—in this case, your boss's thoughts and actions—finding a resolution to your situation is easier. Sometimes, validation alone helps to reduce the stress caused by a micromanaging boss. Be kind to yourself and do not make *her* problem your problem. However, it may be to your advantage to consider some potential suggestions.

So, what is the best way to respond or interact with a micromanager?

Ways to work with a micromanaging boss:

1. *By openly communicating*: Approach your boss and express your concerns about the micromanaging behavior in a respectful and non-confrontational manner. Let her know how it is impacting your work and productivity. While challenging, attempt not to put her in a defensive position.

2. *By setting clear expectations*: Communicate your understanding of the tasks and responsibilities assigned to you and ask for clear guidelines and expectations so your boss feels secure in your abilities. To help Micromanaging Leaders

feel secure, showing them respect and support, being reliable and consistent, listening to their concerns, and validating their feelings or opinions where appropriate are important. You can further contribute to their sense of security by communicating openly and honestly.

3. *By providing regular updates*: Keep your boss informed about your progress and any significant developments. This can help her feel more at ease and reduce the need for constant oversight.

4. *By seeking feedback*: Ask for specific feedback on your work so that you can address any concerns your boss may have and demonstrate your competence and ability to work independently. Imagine going four years without any feedback, assessments, or evaluations. How can a boss justify the work of staff members if she never takes the time or has respect enough to evaluate their performance and provide feedback? Influential leaders guide, mentor, and advise their staff, leading by example. Feedback is priceless information and a way to grow both personally and professionally. It is a gift of knowledge. The value of feedback lies in its ability to provide you with insights, perspectives, and suggestions for improvement. Feedback can help identify strengths and weaknesses, clarify expectations, and guide decision-making. It also fosters open communication, promotes learning and growth, and ultimately contributes to the growth of the employee, boss, and even the company. Whether it's constructive criticism or positive reinforcement, feedback can be a valuable tool for continuous improvement and success. Every true leader should provide feedback to employees. Even better, every leader should request that the employees provide feedback to them.

5. *By offering solutions*: Propose a plan for working more autonomously while keeping your boss informed of your progress and any important updates. Ensure that her expectations are clear and work diligently on her desired projects in order of importance to her. If you have insights she may be unaware of, share potential solutions with her, offering a few and allowing her to choose, validating her security.

6. *By building trust*: Demonstrate your reliability and competence by consistently delivering high-quality work and meeting deadlines. Understand that her control issue is a problem with her, not you or your work. Continue to perform at your best without allowing her management to detract from the content or output of your work. Let her realize your diligence and perseverance, building trust in your ability to "make her look good" through your exemplary performance.

7. *By taking initiative:* Show your boss that you are proactive and capable of making decisions independently. This can help alleviate her need to micromanage every aspect of your work.

8. *By staying organized*: Keep detailed records of your work and progress to show your boss that you are on top of your responsibilities. This will allow efficient access to your work and may help alleviate her need to constantly check in on you.

9. *By acceptance*: Choosing to continue as things are is certainly a choice. Yet, if you choose to remain in the same circumstance, you need to be accountable for this "action" and make the best of it. Accepting being micromanaged does not allow for complaints or negative attitudes. Move to acceptance and find ways to continue to be an effective employee. Set boundaries for yourself and know where your limits are. Work hard and be diligent in all you do, but do not allow yourself to be pushed

beyond your boundaries. Lead by your resilient example and grow both personally and professionally during this process. Perhaps by your consistent example and tireless efforts, your leader may grow as well. You will know if there is a time you need to make a change, such as moving toward one of the following steps. Never lower your standards at any time.

10. *By seeking support*: If the micromanaging behavior persists, consider seeking support from HR or a higher-level manager to help address the issue. Once you have exhausted the suggestions provided, it is reasonable to approach your boss's boss in a non-confrontational manner. Ensure your intentions are to improve your working relationship and promote a positive future environment. Keep in mind this may not always be effective. In the example provided, not only was my boss an ineffective, jealous, and insecure "leader," but the pattern of ineffective and untrained leaders flowed right up the food chain. After all, they were the ones who hired her as a manager to begin with. This leads to the next point.

11. *By respectfully resigning:* When you have exhausted all other possibilities and are sure there are no other alternatives, the next best step may be to resign from this atmosphere and go where you are appreciated. Embrace the possibilities of a new company, position, or even field! Pour your motivation and determination into something new and exciting where you can share your talents, insights, and incredible work ethic in a place where you are appreciated, not just tolerated. Give the proper notice and timeframe of your departure. And if offered an exit interview, take full advantage of *objectively* sharing your experience.

Some leaders may micromanage because they have a need for control and struggle to delegate tasks to others. They may also lack trust in their team members' abilities, leading them to feel the need to monitor and direct every aspect of their work closely. Some leaders may have perfectionist tendencies and believe they are the only ones who can ensure that tasks are completed to their standards. Ultimately, micromanaging can result from a combination of personality traits, insecurities, and a lack of confidence in themselves and others. In general, when dealing with a micromanager or any other type of ineffective leader, document what is occurring and what steps you have taken in an effort to achieve a positive resolution. While journaling could trigger your mind to new and creative ideas to pursue resolution, it could also serve as a peace of mind record if you decide on a career change. And from a legal standpoint, you can never document too much!

You may have heard of the adage: *knowledge is power*. There is a lot of truth to it. With knowledge comes confidence, which can lead to many powerful and successful outcomes. Where possible, it is beneficial to build confidence in others. You will find your own confidence increasing as you do. You may not always have the means and ability to offer all of the following suggestions. However, allow yourself to grow in confidence-building where an opportunity exists, including your family setting. This allows for a more productive and inspiring environment. It is a win-win move.

Ways to build confidence in others:

1. *By encouragement*: Offer positive and supportive feedback to boost confidence and belief in others.
2. *By recognition*: Acknowledge their achievements and efforts to show that you value and appreciate their capabilities.

3. *By empowerment*: Provide opportunities for them to take on new challenges and responsibilities and trust them to make decisions and solve problems independently.
4. *By positive reinforcement*: Use praise and affirmation to reinforce their strengths and successes.
5. *By setting realistic goals*: Help them set achievable goals and provide support and guidance to help them reach those goals.
6. *By providing resources*: Offer access to tools, training, and resources to help them develop new skills and knowledge.
7. *By leading by example*: Demonstrate confidence and self-assurance in your own actions and decisions to inspire and motivate them.
8. *By providing constructive feedback*: Offer constructive criticism and guidance to help them improve and grow while still highlighting their strengths.
9. *By creating a supportive environment*: Foster a positive environment where people feel safe participating, sharing ideas, and taking risks without fear of judgment.
10. *By being a mentor*: Serve as a mentor and coach, providing guidance, advice, support, or even an example as they navigate challenges and develop their confidence.

A boss can also benefit from a boost of confidence. In this case, you will as well! Consider different ways you can indirectly help your boss grow in her abilities. This is a selfless act for her benefit, yet you will also reap the rewards.

Ways to build your boss's confidence in you:

1. *Show initiative and take on new challenges*: Proactively seek out new projects and responsibilities to demonstrate your capabilities and leadership skills.
2. *Provide solutions, not just problems*: When presenting issues or challenges, come prepared with potential solutions or ideas for addressing them.
3. *Communicate effectively*: Be clear and direct in your communication, and provide regular updates on your progress and accomplishments.
4. *Seek feedback and act on it*: Ask your boss for feedback on your performance and areas for improvement, and take action to address any concerns or suggestions.
5. *Be reliable and trustworthy*: Consistently follow through on your commitments and responsibilities and demonstrate integrity in your actions and decisions.
6. *Show strong work ethics*: Demonstrate a strong work ethic and dedication to your job.
7. *Support your boss's goals and priorities*: Understand your boss's objectives and work to align your efforts with her vision and direction for the team or organization.
8. *Be a team player*: Collaborate with your colleagues and support the team's overall success, demonstrating that you can work well with others and contribute to a positive work environment.
9. *Show confidence in your own abilities*: Demonstrate self-assurance and belief in your skills and expertise while being open to learning and growth opportunities. Ensure your self-

assurance does not resemble arrogance. Remain humble yet confident.

10. *Take ownership of your work*: Be accountable for your performance and outcomes and demonstrate that you can be trusted to deliver results.
11. *Build a strong professional relationship*: Invest time in getting to know your boss, understanding her leadership style and preferences, and building a positive and respectful working relationship.

Not all leaders fit into one nicely defined category. As a matter of fact, this is probably a rare occurrence for any boss. In the example described in this chapter, even more so than her ineffective and micromanaging leadership style, stemming from a mixture of insecurity and pressure from upper management, was the growing issue of jealousy once she finally took notice of how effectively the clinics were run without any instruction or guidance from her, which again was her own choosing. A further look at jealousy in leadership is discussed in the following chapter.

Highlighted Character Quality:

Discernment:

What is discernment, and how does it fit into leadership? Discernment is the ability to judge and make good decisions by distinguishing between different options, ideas, or situations. It involves using good judgment, critical thinking, and intuition to make wise choices. Discernment can also refer to the process of seeking guidance or understanding through careful consideration and reflection.

Discernment is an important quality for leaders to grasp, as it allows them to make well-informed and wise decisions. In leadership, discernment is used in several ways. Leaders use discernment to carefully consider all options and choose the best course of action for their team or organization. This involves being able to see through the noise and distractions to identify the most beneficial path forward. Leaders also need to be able to discern the root causes of problems and find effective solutions. This involves using critical thinking skills and the ability to separate relevant information from irrelevant details.

Discernment is also crucial in setting a clear and inspiring vision for the future. Leaders must be able to discern the needs and aspirations of their team or organization and articulate a compelling vision that aligns with those needs. Navigating conflicts and disagreements within their team requires discernment as well. They need to be able to discern the underlying issues and work toward finding a resolution that benefits everyone involved.

Discernment is also essential in identifying and developing talent within the organization. Leaders must be able to discern the strengths and weaknesses of their team members and provide opportunities for growth and development. Discernment is a crucial skill for leaders, allowing them to make sound decisions, solve problems effectively, and lead their teams toward success.

Benefits of discernment:

1. *Better decision-making*: Discernment allows you to understand your options better and make informed choices, leading to better outcomes.

2. *Improved relationships*: Discernment helps you understand the intentions and motivations of others, leading to more meaningful and authentic connections.
3. *Personal growth*: Developing discernment can lead to increased self-awareness and self-reflection, encouraging personal growth and development.
4. *Reduced stress and anxiety*: Accurate assessment of situations and people can reduce the uncertainty and worry that often accompany decision-making.
5. *Enhanced problem-solving skills*: Discernment enables you to identify and understand underlying issues, leading to more effective problem-solving.
6. *Increased confidence*: The ability to discern and understand complex situations can boost self-confidence and self-worth.
7. *Better judgment*: Discernment can help you avoid making impulsive or rash decisions, leading to better judgment and outcomes.
8. *Greater emotional insight*: Discernment enables you to better understand and manage your emotions, as well as those of others.
9. *Increased resilience*: Developing discernment can help you better navigate challenging situations and setbacks, leading to increased resilience and adaptability.
10. *Alignment with personal values and goals*: Discernment helps you make choices that align with your values and long-term goals, leading to a more fulfilling and purposeful life.

While not all leaders may understand and use discernment effectively, it is also vital as an employee to seek discernment in your role. If you are dealing with an ineffective boss or management, the ability to discern may help you understand inconsistencies in their leadership and help you navigate the situation better. You will become a better employee with a greater understanding of the reality of your management situation.

Ways an employee can use discernment when faced with ineffective leadership:

1. Identify the root causes of ineffective leadership, such as lack of communication, unclear expectations, or poor decision-making.
2. Assess the impact of ineffective leadership on your work and the overall team dynamics.
3. Determine the best course of action to address the situation, whether it involves seeking clarification from the leader, offering constructive feedback, or finding alternative ways to achieve your goals.
4. Exercise sound judgment and make informed decisions in your work despite the challenges of ineffective leadership.
5. Cultivate a strong sense of self-awareness and emotional insight to manage your reactions and responses to the situation.

Overall, discernment can empower you to navigate the complexities of ineffective leadership and make the best choices for you and your work. There are many ways you can improve your own ability to discern.

Ways to develop or improve your ability to discern:

1. *Practice critical thinking*: Engage in activities that challenge you to analyze and evaluate information, such as puzzles, debates, or decision-making scenarios. Learn critical thinking skills using practical applications, as found in the book *Who Connects Your Dots?*
2. *Seek diverse perspectives*: Expose yourself to various viewpoints and opinions to understand different angles on an issue. Perform extensive research and collect as much data as possible. Analyze and evaluate the data from each perspective. Be objective in your analysis.
3. *Develop your knowledge and expertise*: An in-depth understanding of a subject matter can help you discern more effectively by allowing you to identify inaccuracies or inconsistencies.
4. *Be open-minded and curious*: Approach new information with a willingness to "learn and discern." Question assumptions. Be objective and consider each alternative.
5. *Evaluate sources of information*: Learn to assess the credibility and reliability of the sources you rely on for information. Be selective and ensure that the sources are trustworthy.
6. *Reflect on your own biases and assumptions*: Understanding your own preconceptions can help you recognize when they might be influencing your judgment. Be mindful of your thoughts and ensure you are objective.
7. *Practice mindfulness*: Cultivate the ability to be present and observant, which can help you notice subtle cues and patterns. Be alert and insightful.

8. *Seek feedback*: Ask for input from others to gain different perspectives and challenge your own thinking. Listen from an unbiased position and consider the feedback objectively with a mindset of improvement and effective outcomes.

9. *Develop your intuition*: Pay attention to your instincts and gut feelings, and also learn to differentiate between intuition and bias. Remember to first go to the source of your thoughts and "Reprogram Your Pre-Program," as described in the book *Elevate Your Mind to Success*.

10. *Continuously learn and grow*: Stay curious and open to new ideas, and be willing to revise your opinions as you gain new information and insights. Continue to read, learn, actively listen, and grow daily. Never stop learning.

Highlighted Leadership Skill:

Effective Communication:

What is effective communication, and how does it fit into leadership? Communication is the process of exchanging information, ideas, thoughts, and feelings between individuals or groups. It can be verbal, nonverbal, written, or visual and is essential for conveying messages, building relationships, and understanding others. *Effective* communication involves active listening, clear expression, and the ability to interpret and respond accurately to the communication of others.

Effective communication is crucial for leadership for several reasons. It allows leaders to clearly communicate their vision, goals, and expectations to their team members. This helps align everyone toward a common goal and ensures everyone understands their role and responsibilities. When leaders communicate effectively, they build trust and credibility with their team members. Open and honest communication fosters a sense of transparency and authenticity, which is essential for building strong relationships and gaining the team's trust.

Effective communication skills enable leaders to address and resolve conflicts within the team. By listening to different perspectives and communicating effectively, leaders can help mitigate misunderstandings and find constructive solutions to conflicts. Through open and transparent communication, leaders can better motivate and inspire their team members. By using clear and persuasive communication, leaders can convey their vision and motivate their team to work toward common goals with enthusiasm and commitment.

Good communication fosters collaboration among team members. Leaders who communicate effectively can encourage open dialogue, exchange of ideas, and teamwork, leading to better problem-solving and innovation within the team. Effective communication enables leaders to provide constructive feedback to their team members. This helps guide and develop their skills, improve performance, and foster a culture of continuous improvement. *Effective* communication is essential for leadership as it helps create a positive and productive work environment, build strong relationships, and achieve common goals.

Benefits of effective communication:

1. *Improved relationships*: Effective communication fosters better understanding and trust between people, leading to stronger and more positive relationships.

2. *Increased productivity*: Clear and open communication helps to avoid misunderstandings and allows for more efficient collaboration and coordination among team members.
3. *Enhanced problem-solving*: When communication is effective, you are better able to express your ideas and concerns, leading to more thorough and effective problem-solving.
4. *Better decision-making*: Effective communication ensures that all relevant information is shared and understood, leading to better-informed and more strategic decision-making.
5. *Reduced conflicts*: Clear and open communication can help prevent and resolve conflicts by addressing issues and concerns in a timely and constructive manner.
6. *Improved morale*: When you feel your voice is heard and your concerns are addressed, you can experience higher morale and job satisfaction.
7. *Greater innovation:* Effective communication encourages sharing diverse perspectives and ideas, leading to a more creative and innovative work environment.
8. *Enhanced customer satisfaction*: Effective communication with customers leads to a better understanding of their needs and concerns, ultimately leading to higher levels of satisfaction and loyalty.
9. *Better leadership*: Effective communication is a key attribute of strong leadership, as it allows leaders to inspire and motivate their team members and to effectively convey their vision and goals.
10. *Personal growth*: Effective communication can lead to improved self-awareness, empathy, and emotional insight, ultimately contributing to personal growth and development.

As you are aware, not all leaders embrace or possess good communication techniques. You may need to lead by example and communicate as effectively as possible, even if it is a one-sided interaction. Your boss may grow in the process and sense the effectiveness of your interactions.

Ways to effectively communicate with an ineffective boss:

1. *Identify the issue*: Before approaching your boss, it's important to identify the specific areas where communication is ineffective. This will help you to address the problem more effectively.

2. *Choose the right time and place*: Find a time when your boss is not stressed or busy, and ask for a private meeting to discuss your concerns. This will ensure that she is more receptive to your feedback.

3. *Be respectful and diplomatic*: When communicating with your boss, it's important to be respectful and diplomatic. Avoid being confrontational or aggressive, and instead, approach the conversation with a calm and professional demeanor.

4. *Provide specific examples*: When discussing the issues with your boss, tactfully provide specific examples of her ineffective communication and how it has impacted your work. This will help her to understand the problem more clearly.

5. *Offer solutions*: Instead of just pointing out the problems, offer potential solutions to improve communication. This will show your boss you are proactive and willing to work with her to resolve the issue. Be professional and diplomatic in your approach, and you may even choose to do this more subtly. Document your efforts.

6. *Seek feedback*: Ask your boss for feedback on how you can better communicate with her. This will show that you are open to improving your own communication skills and are willing to work collaboratively.

7. *Follow up: After the initial conversation, follow up with your boss to see if communication has improved. This will show that you are serious about the issue and* committed to finding a resolution.

8. *Seek support*: If the situation does not improve, consider seeking support from HR or a higher-level manager to address the communication issues with your boss. Sometimes, an outside perspective can help to facilitate a resolution.

You can only do so much when involved with an ineffective communicator. Something else you can always do is work to improve yourself. There are many ways to improve your own communication skills.

Ways to develop or improve your communication skills:

1. *Actively listen to others*: Pay attention to what the other person is saying without interrupting or thinking of your response. This shows respect and understanding. Ensure you are focused on hearing and comprehending the message rather than thinking about what you will say next.

2. *Practice empathy*: Try understanding the other person's perspective, feelings, and intentions. This can help build rapport and trust in communication. Put yourself in their shoes, so to speak.

3. *Be clear and concise*: Convey your message using simple and direct language. Avoid using jargon or complex language that

may confuse the listener. Choosing a complex approach may actually cost you credibility. Keep it simple, stupid (KISS).

4. *Use nonverbal communication effectively*: To convey your message effectively, pay attention to your body language, facial expressions, and tone of voice. Use positive body language. Maintain eye contact, use open and welcoming gestures, and be aware of the inflection in your voice.

5. *Ask for feedback*: Seek feedback from others on your communication style and areas for improvement. This can help you identify blind spots and make necessary adjustments. You may even try videotaping yourself in conversation to learn more about your style or any peculiarities you may find.

6. *Practice active communication*: Regularly engage in conversations and discussions to hone your communication skills. This can be done through public speaking, group discussions, or one-on-one conversations.

7. *Read and educate yourself*: Stay informed and educated on various topics to broaden your knowledge and vocabulary, which can improve your communication skills. Learn from observation and even seek charismatic examples to emulate.

8. *Be open-minded*: Be open to different perspectives and ideas, and be willing to adapt your communication style to accommodate others.

9. *Build rapport*: Establish a connection with others by finding common ground, showing genuine interest, and being positively approachable.

10. *Avoid assumptions*: Clarify any misunderstandings and ask for interpretation if needed. Avoid making assumptions about what others are thinking or feeling.

11. *Practice assertiveness*: Learn to express your thoughts and feelings directly and respectfully while also being open to the thoughts and feelings of others.

12. *Seek out training or coaching*: Consider taking communication skills workshops or working with a communication coach to improve your skills.

Good communication is essential in all aspects of life, including personal relationships, business interactions, and professional success. It allows you to express your thoughts and ideas effectively, understand the perspectives of others, and build strong connections. Clear and open communication can prevent misunderstandings, conflicts, and mistakes, leading to better collaboration, problem-solving, and overall productivity. Sharp communication skills are highly valued in the workplace and can contribute to career advancement and success. Communicating effectively is crucial for building strong relationships, achieving goals, and fostering positive interactions in all areas of life. Strive for continual improvements in effectively communicating with others.

Reflect:

1. Have you ever worked for a micromanaging boss? How did you deal with this type of behavior? What were the results? What did you do correctly?

2. What changes will you make as a result of this chapter? What is your desired outcome?

3. Where does the micromanaging behavior stem from? Is it solely with your immediate boss, or is it with the company's

management in general? What will you do if the issue is only with your boss? What will you do if it is company-wide?

4. What are some dangers of a micromanaging leader? What can you do when faced with this situation? What can you add to the list provided in this chapter?

5. What do you know about discernment? How can discernment be used effectively in leadership? Describe a time when you lacked discernment. Describe a time when you showed discernment despite challenges. Compare and contrast each example. What do you notice?

6. Find ways to program discernment into your "preprogram." More information about how to "Reprogram Your Pre-program" is found in *Elevate Your Mind to Success, Success Is EleMENTAL*, and at www.ABookinTime.net.

7. Describe *effective* communication. How is this used effectively as a leader? How can it be used effectively as an employee?

8. Rate your current ability to communicate well with others. What are you doing correctly? How can you improve?

9. What are some benefits of effective communication? How can this be applied to a situation involving a micromanaging boss?

10. Research more about discernment and effective communication and practice these valuable skills daily.

CHAPTER 5
The Jealous Leader

A jealous leader is like a storm that destroys everything in its path, unable to see the goodness, value, and potential in others.

—Jill Fandrich

A jealous boss can poison the atmosphere of an entire workplace, creating a culture of mistrust and competition instead of collaboration and growth.

—Jill Fandrich

The unfortunateness of having a jealous boss can negatively impact you in many ways, including the environment. A jealous boss may create a toxic work environment by constantly undermining and belittling his employees, leading to low morale and decreased productivity. He may unfairly favor certain employees over others, creating a sense of inequality and unfairness within the workplace. A jealous leader may be overly suspicious and untrusting of his employees, leading to a lack of open communication and collaboration.

Employees may even find their career growth hindered by a jealous boss unwilling to support their professional development and advancement within the company. The consequences of a jealous boss can lead to high turnover rates as employees seek a healthier work environment. As described, working for a jealous boss can significantly impact the well-being and success of both the employees and the company as a whole.

Many years ago, I worked in a hospital and enjoyed all of the employees, peers, and even management staff. I was able to spend time with patients and found myself rewarded by the collaboration and professionalism in the surrounding environment, or so I thought. The camaraderie with my peers and even my own subordinates was pleasant and even desirable. I truly enjoyed my work and interaction with patients, and I looked forward to working every day and even accepted extra shifts when offered. What I failed to see was the jealousy that had been developing within my boss toward me, my work, and my relationships with others.

I finally decided to pursue my doctorate after practicing in my field for a few years. As an employee of this facility, according to the company rules and benefits, I was entitled to a certain reimbursement for further education related to my field. I was already a registered pharmacist and was pursuing a doctor of pharmacy degree, which was the next advancement step. I approached my boss with this information and my desire to fulfill this goal of mine. My boss looked me right in the eyes and said, "*A doctor of pharmacy degree has nothing to do with pharmacy.*" Needless to say, I was speechless. I was confused and even wondered if the show *Candid Camera* was filming again! I clearly conveyed my confusion, and he repeated, "*A doctor of pharmacy degree has nothing to do with pharmacy, so the funding and reimbursement are not approved.*" He then dismissed me from his office.

Have you ever worked for a company with a boss jealous of your abilities, looks, or charisma? Have you ever been held back or overlooked for a promotion due to *his* insecurities? What was the scenario? Were you acting appropriately? Did you cause any of the turmoil? Was the tension just between you and the boss? Or were there other people affected as well? How did you respond to the situation?

Depending on your particular situation, there are some ideas you can try to remedy the circumstances. First, consider what you have already tried and the outcome of the attempt. Was it effective? Why do you think it was or was not effective?

Ways to deal with a jealous boss:

1. *Communicate openly and honestly*: Address the issue with your boss in a calm and respectful manner. Tell him how his behavior affects you and ask for feedback on improving the situation. Diplomatically ask questions regarding his decision and ensure you have a fact-finding mindset, absent of accusations. With pure intentions, seek to find the basis of the reason for the decision. Collect as much information as you can. It is important to address this as soon as possible. Recall the communication techniques discussed in the previous chapter and incorporate them into your discussions.

2. *Clarify expectations*: Ensure you understand your boss's expectations and work to meet them. This can help alleviate feelings of insecurity or jealousy. Examine your work, consider your responsibilities, and ensure you complete all your tasks to the best of your abilities. You may even want to stretch above and beyond them to leave no room for unnecessary criticism.

3. *Be transparent*: Ensure processes align with your boss's methods in all your work. An insecure boss may be "hypercritical" and would benefit from your transparency. Being transparent can lead to several benefits in the workplace. It

can help build trust, as he will appreciate your honesty and openness. This can create a more positive and productive working relationship. Transparency can lead to better and more objective decision-making. When you are open about your thoughts, concerns, and challenges, your boss can offer unbiased guidance and support to help you address issues more effectively. This can ultimately lead to better outcomes as well. Additionally, transparency can help you receive constructive feedback and recognition for your work. By openly sharing your accomplishments, challenges, and goals with your boss, you can create opportunities for growth and development.

4. *Be supportive*: Offer to help your boss with his workload or take on additional responsibilities to show your dedication and commitment to the team. A jealous personality can be challenging as there is a chance this may "rub him the wrong way." Use your best judgment, yet err on the side of offering more support.

5. *Seek feedback and advice*: Ask for feedback on your performance and seek advice on how to improve. This can help build trust and demonstrate your willingness to grow and develop. It can also provide insight into how your boss currently assesses your performance. Pay close attention to the feedback and evaluations and address every issue or concern. Document all you have done to address his feedback.

6. *Stay professional*: Keep your interactions with your boss professional and diplomatic, and maintain a positive attitude. Avoid gossiping or negative behavior.

7. *Build trust*: Show your boss that you are trustworthy and reliable. "Humbly" keep him informed about your work and accomplishments to build confidence in your abilities.

8. *Build a support network*: Seek support from colleagues, mentors, or HR if the situation becomes unmanageable. A support network can help you navigate the challenges of working with a jealous boss.

9. *Document interactions*: Keep a detailed record of any concerning interactions or behavior from your boss. This can be useful if you need to escalate the situation to HR or higher management. It is always beneficial to keep a record of your achievements and progress as well. This will serve as a record of your performance and your value to the team and the company.

10. *Consider your options*: If the situation does not improve and becomes intolerable or even toxic, consider looking for other job opportunities within the company or externally. Sometimes, another person's insecurities are beyond what you can overcome. Your well-being and mental health should be a priority. You have valuable abilities to offer, and a reputable company with a seasoned leader would benefit from your skill set.

In the previous story, after confronting my boss respectfully one more time and still receiving a no-funding answer, I set up an appointment with *his* boss and presented the same question to her. I was already following most of the *ways to deal with a jealous boss*, and this was the next logical step. She said excitedly that I qualified for the funding with the degree I mentioned. She was thrilled at my ambition and eager for me to start the program. I thanked her for her time and information and casually mentioned that my boss had declined the funding and that I just wanted to verify the answer.

Working for a boss who isn't a true leader is difficult. While it still can be done, I realized my boss was threatened by my ambition, skills, determination, charisma, and even my youth. I had never considered any of these things before his prejudice revealed his jealousy and insecurities. He was the one with the problem, and it was up to him to work on his own insecurities. When my eyes were opened, I turned in my two-week resignation, immediately hired into a management position elsewhere, and pursued my doctorate. As a funny side note, that boss immediately registered for the same doctorate program, received full funding, and graduated a semester after me.

What are some reasons a boss may be jealous of you?

Reasons a boss may be jealous:

1. You are more skilled or talented than the boss in a certain area.
2. You receive recognition and praise from higher-ups or clients.
3. You have a better relationship with colleagues or clients.
4. You are more successful or accomplished in your work than the boss.
5. You have a better work-life balance and seem happier and more fulfilled.
6. You receive more attention or support from the higher-ups.
7. You have a better rapport with the team and are seen as a natural leader.
8. You are more innovative and creative in your approach to work.

9. You are more respected and admired by colleagues and clients.
10. You have a better ability to handle difficult situations or challenges.
11. The boss has insecurities that are not dealt with.
12. The boss isn't applying himself as he could be and fears the stability of his position.
13. The boss lacks leadership skills.

Remember, a jealous boss is the one with the problem, not you. Ways have been examined to continue to work with a jealous boss to increase the chances of a better relationship. However, it is impossible to change someone; leading by example is the best you can do. Ultimately, you must do what is best for you regarding your health and happiness. Weigh the pros and cons of your circumstances. Take time to write them out and evaluate each side. What scenario are you able to live with? Which one gives you peace of mind and the ability to sleep soundly? What would it take to achieve contentment in your work environment? What are you willing to change? What are you not willing to change? What are your boundaries when dealing with a jealous boss?

Highlighted Character Quality:

Contentment:

What is contentment, and how does it fit into leadership? Contentment is a state of being mentally and emotionally satisfied with your life and circumstances. It involves feeling a sense of peace, fulfillment, and happiness, regardless of external factors or material possessions. Contentment is often associated with gratitude, acceptance, and a positive mindset.

Contentment fits in leadership by promoting a sense of inner peace and fulfillment, which can positively impact decision-making, communication, and relationships with others. A content leader is more likely to inspire trust and confidence in his team, as he is able to approach challenges with a calm and balanced mindset. Additionally, contentment can help a leader maintain a long-term perspective and stay focused on his values and goals, even in the face of adversity. Contentment in leadership can lead to greater resilience, empathy, and the ability to motivate and inspire others.

What are the dynamics of contentment in dealing with ineffective leaders? Is it possible to still be content with a challenging leader?

Ways to be content despite adversity with a boss:

1. *Focus on what you can control*: Instead of getting frustrated with your boss's behavior, focus on what you can control, such as your own attitude, work ethic, growth, and response to difficult situations.
2. *Set boundaries*: To protect your mental and emotional well-being, establish clear boundaries with your boss. This may involve politely declining any unreasonable requests or limiting your availability outside work hours.
3. *Seek support*: Reach out to colleagues, friends, or a mentor for support and advice. A support system can help you navigate difficult situations and provide a sounding board for your frustrations.
4. *Practice self-care*: Take care of yourself both physically and mentally. Engage in activities that bring you joy, such

as exercising, spending time with loved ones, or pursuing hobbies. This can help you maintain a positive mindset and reduce stress. Allow yourself to have fun! Take a detox bath and recharge your body, mind, and spirit. What other activities do you find relaxing?

5. *Communicate effectively*: Try to communicate with your boss in a calm and respectful manner. Express your concerns and seek clarification on expectations. Effective communication can help minimize misunderstandings and reduce tension. How would you rate your current communication with your boss? What are you doing correctly? How can you improve?

6. *Focus on the positive*: Look for the silver lining in your situation. Focus on the aspects of your job you enjoy and the skills you develop. This can help shift your perspective and reduce the impact of a difficult boss on your overall happiness.

7. *Participate in team unity*: Hopefully, you are already a team player. Be even more intentional about collaborating with your peers and other company personnel. Perhaps allow your unit to be the focus rather than standing out to a challenging boss. This will create a more favorable environment for you to thrive in and work on your own professional growth.

8. *Explore other options*: If the situation becomes unbearable, consider exploring other job opportunities. Prioritize your mental and emotional well-being; sometimes, a change in environment may be necessary for your own professional growth and happiness. Weigh out the pros and cons and give each thoughtful consideration.

Contentment is an essential character quality to build into your mindset. Make it a habit. It doesn't mean everything in your life must be perfect. You can be content *despite* your circumstances. It is a *choice*.

Benefits of being content:

1. *Peace of mind*: Contentment brings a sense of inner peace and calm, allowing you to feel less stressed and anxious.
2. *Improved mental health*: Contentment can lead to better mental health as it reduces the risk of depression and anxiety.
3. *Better relationships*: When you are content, you are more likely to be satisfied with your relationships and less likely to seek validation from others.
4. *Increased resilience*: Contentment helps you develop resilience, making it easier to handle life's challenges and setbacks.
5. *Enhanced physical health*: Contentment has been linked to better physical health, including lower blood pressure and a stronger immune system.
6. *Greater productivity*: When you are content, you are more focused and motivated, leading to increased productivity at work and in other areas of your life. You have an extra passion and openness to accomplish more. Energy is transformed from negative to positive, leading to more productivity and favorable outcomes.
7. *Improved decision-making*: Contentment allows you to make decisions from a place of clarity and calm rather than from a place of stress or dissatisfaction. When your mind is decluttered and more open to processing information, both your conscious and subconscious minds can participate, leading to more solutions and creative options.

8. *Increased happiness*: Contentment is a key factor in overall happiness and life satisfaction.

Ways to develop or improve contentment:

1. *Practice gratitude*: Take time each day to think about and write down what and who you are grateful for. This can help shift your focus from what you lack to what you have.
2. *Focus on the present*: Instead of dwelling on the past or worrying about the future, try to stay present and appreciate the moment.
3. *Cultivate mindfulness*: Engage in mindfulness practices such as meditation or deep breathing exercises to help you stay present and reduce stress. Look and listen to your surroundings. What do you notice?
4. *Set realistic goals*: Instead of constantly chasing after unattainable goals, set realistic and achievable goals for yourself. This can help you feel a sense of accomplishment and satisfaction. As you become more and more content, you can expand your goals even more and enjoy the adventure.
5. *Focus on what you can control*: Shift your mind from focusing on things you cannot control to things you can. For example, you cannot control other people's actions or even their way of thinking, nor should you! Focus instead on your actions and be accountable to them alone. Lead by example and positively affect others through your actions. Let go of things beyond your control.
6. *Surround yourself with positive people*: Spend time with people who lift you up and make you feel good about yourself. Positive energy is infectious. Enjoy the ambition and drive that

are emulated by the positive energy. Ensure these people positively affect your growth and not just affirm a complaint you may have.

7. *Take care of your physical health*: Exercise regularly, eat a balanced diet, get adequate sleep, and stay hydrated. Physical health can significantly impact your mental well-being. Boost your natural immunity, as your body's own immunity is the best defense against diseases and infections.

8. *Limit social media and screen time*: Constantly comparing yourself to others on social media can lead to feelings of inadequacy. Limit your time on social media and electronic stimulation. Focus on real-life connections and experiences.

9. *Seek professional help if needed*: If you are struggling with feelings of discontentment, consider seeking help from a therapist or counselor. They can provide support and guidance to help you work through your challenges.

Highlighted Leadership Skill:

Delegation:

What is delegation, and how does it fit into leadership? Delegation is the process of assigning tasks, responsibilities, and authority to another person or group in order to achieve a specific goal or outcome. It involves empowering others to take on certain tasks and make decisions on behalf of the delegator while still retaining overall accountability for the outcome. Delegation is an important skill for effective leadership and management, as it allows leaders to focus on higher-level tasks, disseminate the workload, and enable the development of others within an organization.

Delegation fits into leadership by allowing leaders to effectively distribute tasks and responsibilities among their team members. By delegating tasks, leaders can empower their team, develop their skills, and promote a sense of ownership and accountability. Delegation also allows leaders to focus on higher-level strategic tasks and decision-making rather than getting bogged down in day-to-day operational details. Effective delegation is a key component of successful leadership, as it allows leaders to leverage the strengths and capabilities of their team to achieve organizational goals.

Ways a leader can delegate:

1. *Task delegation*: The leader can assign specific tasks to team members based on their skills and expertise.
2. *Authority delegation*: The leader can empower team members to make decisions and take responsibility for certain aspects of a project or process.
3. *Responsibility delegation*: The leader can assign team members specific responsibilities, such as overseeing a particular area of the project or managing a certain aspect of the team's work.
4. *Time management delegation*: The leader can allocate time and resources to team members to ensure tasks are completed efficiently and effectively.
5. *Decision-making delegation*: The leader can involve team members in the decision-making process and delegate decision-making authority to them when appropriate.
6. *Resource delegation*: The leader can allocate resources such as budget, personnel, and equipment to team members to ensure they have what they need to complete their tasks.

7. *Mentorship delegation*: The leader can delegate the task of mentoring and coaching team members to more experienced team members, encouraging growth and development within the team.

It is also important for employees to become versed in delegation as well. Have you had much experience delegating responsibility or tasks to others? What did this involve? What was the outcome? Delegation is an essential skill for employees to have for several reasons. First, it allows you to manage your workload effectively and prioritize tasks, ensuring all necessary work is completed promptly. Delegation also encourages teamwork and collaboration within the organization, as you can rely on each other to help accomplish common goals. Delegating tasks can also help you develop leadership skills and build trust with your colleagues as you demonstrate your ability to empower others and effectively manage resources. Knowing how to delegate is crucial for being efficient, productive, and successful in your role.

Benefits of delegating:

1. *Increased productivity*: Delegating tasks allows you to focus on high-priority activities while others handle less critical tasks, leading to increased overall productivity.
2. *Development of skills*: Delegating tasks to others can provide them with opportunities to develop new skills and gain experience, leading to a more skilled and capable team.
3. *Time management*: Delegating frees up your time to focus on strategic activities and decision-making, leading to more effective time management.

4. *Empowerment:* Delegating tasks can empower team members to take ownership of their work and feel more engaged and motivated.

5. *Improved efficiency:* Delegating tasks to those best suited to handle them can lead to improved efficiency and quality of work.

6. *Better work-life balance:* Delegating tasks can help reduce your workload and allow you to achieve a better work-life balance.

7. *Building trust:* Delegating tasks can help build trust and strengthen relationships with your team, showing that you have confidence in their abilities.

8. *Focus on strategic activities:* Delegating can free up your time to focus on strategic activities that can have a greater impact on the organization's overall success.

As delegation is an important skill for everyone to learn, how do you improve? Whether you are an employee, leader of a team, or leader in your own home, consider the following ideas for building delegating skills.

Ways to develop or improve delegating skills:

1. *Trust your team:* Recognize the skills and capabilities of your team members and trust them to handle tasks and responsibilities. Avoid micromanaging and encourage them to take ownership of their work and make decisions within their scope of responsibility. Learn to let go once you delegate.

2. *Communicate clearly:* Communicate in a way each team member can understand. When delegating, clearly outline the tasks, deadlines, and desired outcomes to ensure everyone

is on the same page. However, let them figure out "the how" of the task where possible. Be sure to provide any necessary resources or support where possible.

3. *Set clear goals and priorities*: Clearly define the goals and priorities for each task or project you delegate. This will help your team members understand the importance of their work and stay focused on the end result. Prioritize tasks and responsibilities and allocate them to the most suitable team members based on their skills and workload.

4. *Provide necessary resources*: Ensure your team has the necessary resources, information, and support to successfully complete the delegated tasks. Offer training and support to help your team members develop the skills and knowledge needed to do so.

5. *Set up a feedback loop*: Establish regular check-ins and feedback sessions to monitor progress and provide guidance when needed. Let the team know you are there to support them and value their work and input on the project.

6. *Evaluate and learn*: Reflect on the outcomes of your delegations and learn from the experience to improve your delegation skills in the future. Get to know your team members' strengths, weaknesses, and interests. This will help you delegate tasks to individuals best suited for them.

7. *Continuously improve*: Reflect on the feedback you've acquired from your team and seek additional educational resources on how to improve. Continuously work on developing your delegating skills from a variety of sources.

8. *Lead by example*: Demonstrate effective delegation by empowering and trusting your team members and effectively managing your workload. Show your ability to lead in the

decisions you make and how you make them. Exemplify leadership as you collaborate with others and actively listen to different perspectives and feedback.

Delegating is important for several reasons. It allows you to focus on high-priority tasks and responsibilities, which can increase productivity and efficiency within an organization. Delegating to team members enables them to develop new skills and expand their knowledge, ultimately benefiting the organization in the long run. It also empowers team members by giving them a sense of ownership and responsibility, boosting morale and motivation.

Time management is a valuable effect of delegation. Delegating tasks allows you to manage your time more effectively by prioritizing and focusing on tasks requiring expertise and attention. Collaboration and teamwork result from delegation within an organization, as team members work together to achieve common goals. In summary, delegating is essential for creating a more efficient, empowered, and collaborative work environment.

 Reflect:

1. Have you ever worked for a jealous boss? How did you deal with this type of behavior? What were the results? What did you do correctly?

2. What changes will you make as a result of this chapter? What is your desired outcome?

3. Where does the jealousy stem from? Is it solely with your immediate boss, or is there an issue with the company's management in general? What will you do if the issue is only with your boss? What will you do if it is company-wide?

4. What are some dangers of a jealous leader? What can you do when faced with this situation? What can you add to the list provided in this chapter?

5. What do you know about contentment? How can contentment be used effectively in leadership? How can contentment be used as an employee? Describe a time when you lacked contentment in a situation. Describe a time when you were content despite challenging circumstances. Compare and contrast each example. What do you notice?

6. Find ways to program contentment into your "preprogram." More information about how to "Reprogram Your Pre-Program" is found in *Elevate Your Mind to Success, Success Is Ele-MENTAL*, and at www.ABookinTime.net.

7. Describe delegation. How is this used effectively as a leader? How can it be used effectively as an employee?

8. Rate your current ability to delegate. What are you doing correctly? How can you improve?

9. What are some benefits of proper delegation? How can this be applied to a situation involving a jealous boss?

10. Research more about contentment and delegating and practice these valuable skills daily.

CHAPTER 6
The Corrupt, Manipulative, and Divisive Leader

> *Corrupt, manipulative, and divisive leaders are like rotten fruit; their actions may sometimes look good on the outside but are filled with decay and poison on the inside.*
> —Jill Fandrich

> *Sometimes, the bravest and most important thing you can do is to leave a toxic and harmful environment, even if it means walking away from what you once knew. Your well-being and integrity are worth more than any false sense of loyalty.*
> —Jill Fandrich

There are many forms of harmful leadership. For example, manipulative leaders are skilled at manipulating and deceiving others to maintain power and control. Corrupt leaders engage in unethical and illegal behavior, such as embezzlement and bribery, for personal gain. In contrast, divisive leaders sow discord and division within their organization, creating a toxic and dysfunctional work environment.

While it may be dangerous to stick around under corrupt and other harmful leadership, especially if it slithers all the way up the food chain, there are some ideas on how to deal with certain situations. It may be difficult to be the voice of change or even revelation. Only you can decide your level of tolerance, bravery, or even safety under the circumstances. Use your best judgment and think critically about the situation.

Ways to deal with a toxic leader:

1. *Seek support and guidance from trusted colleagues or mentors*: It can be helpful to discuss the situation with others who may have experienced similar challenges and can offer advice on how to navigate them. To report the behavior and seek guidance on handling the situation, contact HR, a trusted colleague, or a higher-up in the company.

2. *Document and report unethical behavior*: Keep a record of any corrupt or manipulative actions, unethical behavior, or inappropriate requests made by your boss and report them to the appropriate authorities, such as HR or a higher-level manager. If conducive to the situation, hold him accountable by reporting his actions to the proper authorities or regulatory bodies.

3. *Challenge the behavior in a respectful and professional manner*: If it feels safe to do so, address the behavior directly with the leader, expressing your concerns and providing examples of how his actions are detrimental to the team or organization. Document your actions and his responses.

4. *Focus on maintaining integrity and ethical conduct*: Lead by example and uphold high standards of conduct, even in the face of corrupt or divisive leadership. Challenge the toxic

leadership by presenting alternative solutions and advocating for change. Document your efforts.

5. *Build alliances and support networks*: Form alliances with other colleagues who may share similar concerns and work together to address the issues and advocate for positive change. Organize and mobilize others to demand transparency and ethical behavior from the leadership. Support and empower whistleblowers who are willing to expose corruption within the leadership.

6. *Consider seeking alternative employment opportunities*: If the situation becomes unbearable and there is no prospect of change, exploring other job opportunities that offer a healthier work environment may be necessary. Create a list of pros and cons about your position in the company and think critically about your future. What is most important to you? Will this position help you achieve your goals and reach your dreams?

7. *Engage in self-care and stress management*: Dealing with corrupt or manipulative leadership can be emotionally and mentally draining. Make sure to prioritize self-care and seek support from friends, family, or a therapist if needed.

8. *Act as an advocate*: Advocate for reforms and policies that promote transparency, accountability, and ethical behavior within the organization or community. Engage in peaceful protests and demonstrations to raise awareness about the toxic leadership and demand change.

9. *Take appropriate legal action*: If the harm induced is severe and affecting your well-being, consider seeking legal advice to understand your rights and options for addressing the situation, perhaps even legal recourse by filing a lawsuit or taking legal action against the corrupt leadership.

10. *Show proper support*: Support and promote ethical leaders committed to honesty, integrity, and good governance.

Manipulative, corrupt, or divisive leaders can be toxic in several ways. Their manipulative behavior can create a toxic work environment, as they may use deceit, coercion, or emotional manipulation to control and exploit their subordinates. This can lead to feelings of distrust, anxiety, and stress among their team members, as well as a lack of psychological safety and a fear of retaliation for speaking out against their leader's actions. Corrupt leaders can breed a culture of unethical behavior within their organization, leading to systemic corruption, fraud, and dishonesty. This can damage the reputation and credibility of the organization, as well as erode trust with stakeholders and the public. Finally, divisive leaders can create a toxic atmosphere of tension, conflict, and division among their team members, as they may pit individuals against each other, encourage competition over collaboration, and foster a culture of fear and insecurity. This can lead to decreased morale, productivity, and overall well-being of the organization. Manipulative, corrupt, or divisive leaders can profoundly and negatively impact the organization, leading to toxicity, dysfunction, and long-term damage to the organization's culture and success.

Your work environment should be a positive atmosphere in which to thrive. You spend a significant portion of your day at work, so make it a priority to enjoy what you do and where you do it. Is it time to make a change? What are your values? What is most important to you in a job or career?

Reasons it's important to enjoy your job:

1. *Job satisfaction*: Enjoying your job can lead to greater job satisfaction, which in turn can lead to better mental and emotional well-being. It can also lead to a greater sense of fulfillment and purpose in your work.
2. *Increased productivity*: When you enjoy your job, you are more likely to be motivated and engaged in your work. This can lead to increased productivity and better performance, benefiting both you and your employer.
3. *Better work-life balance*: Enjoying your job can help you achieve a healthy work-life balance. When you are happy at work, you are less likely to feel stressed and overwhelmed, allowing you to better enjoy your personal life outside of work.
4. *Career growth*: Enjoying your job can lead to greater career growth and development opportunities. When you are motivated and engaged, you are more likely to seek out new challenges and opportunities for advancement.
5. *Positive work environment*: When you enjoy your job, you are more likely to contribute to a positive work environment. This can lead to better relationships with colleagues and a more cohesive and supportive team.
6. *Overall well-being*: Enjoying your job can positively impact your overall well-being. It can lead to lower stress levels, better physical health, and a more positive outlook on life.

Enjoying your job is important for your personal well-being, career growth, and overall satisfaction in life. It can positively impact your professional and personal life, making it essential to a fulfilling and successful career. If you continue to work under manipulative, corrupt, or divisive leadership, you may want to take a step back, evaluate your situation, and reframe your priorities. What is most important to you?

Highlighted Character Quality:

Integrity:

What is integrity, and how does it fit into leadership? Integrity is the quality of being honest and having strong moral principles. It involves doing the right thing even when no one is watching and being consistent in your actions and values. Integrity also includes trustworthiness, ethics, and a strong sense of accountability.

Integrity is crucial in leadership as it helps to build trust and credibility with followers. When leaders demonstrate integrity, they are honest, ethical, and reliable, which helps create a positive and supportive work environment. Integrity also helps leaders make fair and just decisions and act in the best interests of their team and organization. Additionally, leaders with integrity are more likely to inspire and motivate their followers, as they lead by example and uphold high ethical standards. Integrity is essential in leadership as it fosters trust, respect, and loyalty among followers, contributing to the team and company's success.

Benefits of integrity:

1. *Trust:* People are likelier to trust and rely on people who demonstrate integrity in their actions and behavior.
2. *Respect:* Integrity garners respect from others. It shows a strong moral character and a commitment to doing what is right.

3. *Credibility*: Those with integrity are seen as more credible and trustworthy, which can lead to greater opportunities and influence in both personal and professional settings.
4. *Consistency*: Integrity-bearing individuals are more likely to be consistent in their actions and decisions, leading to greater reliability and predictability.
5. *Positive relationships*: Integrity fosters positive and healthy relationships, as it builds a strong foundation of trust and respect.
6. *Personal growth*: Practicing integrity can lead to personal growth and self-improvement, as it requires introspection and a commitment to doing the right thing.
7. *Ethical leadership*: People with integrity are more likely to be effective and ethical leaders, as they set a positive example for others to follow. Integrity will help develop professional growth and build an ethical and trustworthy leadership reputation.
8. *Peace of mind*: Living with integrity can bring a sense of peace and satisfaction, knowing that you are living in alignment with your values and principles.

Maintaining integrity despite a toxic boss is important for several reasons. It allows you to uphold personal values and principles, which can contribute to self-esteem and an overall sense of self-worth. Integrity can also help you build trust and credibility with co-workers and other stakeholders, which is crucial for long-term career success. Furthermore, demonstrating integrity can serve as a form of protection against the negative influence of a toxic boss, as it can provide a moral compass and a sense of control in a challenging work environment. Ultimately, integrity is essential for maintaining a sense of personal and professional integrity, even in the face of adversity.

Ways to show integrity despite poor leadership:

1. *Lead by example*: Demonstrate integrity in your own actions and decisions, setting a positive example for others to follow.
2. *Maintain open communication*: Be transparent and honest with colleagues and team members, even when the leader is not.
3. *Uphold your values*: Stay true to your own values and principles, even in the face of poor leadership. Do not compromise them under any circumstances.
4. *Support and empower others*: Encourage and support your colleagues to also uphold integrity and ethical behavior, creating a positive and cohesive team environment.
5. *Seek feedback and input*: Encourage open dialogue and feedback from others, and be willing to listen and consider alternative perspectives.
6. *Take responsibility*: Hold yourself accountable for your own actions and decisions, and take ownership of your responsibilities, regardless of the leader's behavior.
7. *Advocate for change*: If possible, work toward advocating for leadership or organizational culture changes that promote integrity and ethical behavior.

Integrity can be further developed as a character quality. It is an essential quality to build into your personal and professional life. Strive to incorporate this quality into your mindset.

Ways to develop and improve integrity:

1. Be honest and transparent in all your dealings and interactions with others. Always be truthful.
2. Keep your word and follow through on your commitments.
3. Admit and learn from your mistakes and take responsibility for your actions. Be accountable.
4. Practice ethical and moral behavior in all aspects of your life.
5. Treat others with respect and fairness. Show empathy and compassion.
6. Develop and uphold strong personal values and principles.
7. Stand up for what is right, even when difficult or unpopular.
8. Be consistent in your actions and behaviors.
9. Surround yourself with people of integrity and learn from their example.
10. Continuously work on self-improvement and personal growth.

Integrity is a key value that is vital in both personal and professional lives. Honesty and strong moral principles are essential for building trust and credibility. Integrity is important because it helps build strong relationships in personal and professional settings. It also helps you make ethical decisions and be consistent and reliable in your actions. In the workplace, integrity is essential for creating a positive and ethical work environment and fostering trust and respect among colleagues. Integrity is a fundamental value crucial for living a moral and meaningful life.

Highlighted Leadership Skill:

Time Management:

What is time management, and how does it fit into leadership? Time management is the process of planning and organizing how to divide your time between specific activities. It involves setting goals, prioritizing tasks, and allocating enough time to complete each task effectively. Time management also includes being mindful of how long tasks actually take to complete and making adjustments as necessary. Good time management allows you to be more productive, reduce stress, and have a better work-life balance.

Time management is a crucial skill for effective leadership. Leaders must be able to prioritize tasks, allocate resources, and make efficient use of their time to ensure that they are able to meet their goals and objectives. Time management allows leaders to be more organized, focused, and productive, enabling them to lead better and manage their team or organization. Additionally, effective time management can also help leaders set a good example for their team and create a culture of efficiency and productivity. Leaders who are able to manage their time effectively are more likely to inspire and motivate their team members to do the same.

Benefits of proper time management:

1. *Increased productivity*: Proper time management allows you to prioritize tasks and allocate time effectively, leading to increased productivity and efficiency in completing tasks.
2. *Reduced stress*: When you manage your time effectively and avoid procrastination, you can reduce the stress and anxiety

that often come with feeling overwhelmed by deadlines and responsibilities.

3. *Improved decision-making*: With proper time management, you have the luxury of making well-thought-out decisions rather than rushing through tasks or making impulsive choices due to time constraints.

4. *Better work-life balance*: Proper time management can improve the balance between your professional and personal lives, leading to a happier and healthier lifestyle.

5. *Enhanced focus and concentration*: When you manage your time effectively, you can give your full attention to the task at hand without feeling distracted or overwhelmed by other responsibilities.

6. *Increased opportunities for personal development*: Proper time management allows you to allocate time for personal growth, learning new skills, and pursuing hobbies or interests outside of work.

7. *Improved reputation and reliability*: When you consistently manage your time well, you are seen as reliable, responsible, and trustworthy, leading to improved relationships and opportunities in both personal and professional settings.

Ways leaders use time management:

1. *Setting priorities*: Leaders identify the most important tasks and allocate their time and resources accordingly.

2. *Delegating tasks*: Leaders delegate tasks to team members based on their strengths and availability, allowing them to focus on more critical responsibilities.

3. *Planning and organizing*: Leaders create schedules and plans to ensure their time is used efficiently and effectively.

4. *Avoiding distractions*: Leaders minimize distractions and interruptions to stay focused on their priorities.

5. *Using technology*: Leaders utilize time-saving tools and technology to streamline processes and manage their time more effectively.

6. *Setting boundaries*: Leaders establish clear boundaries to protect their time and energy from being drained by non-essential tasks or requests.

7. *Avoiding multitasking*: Leaders focus on one task at a time to maximize their productivity and effectiveness.

8. *Taking breaks*: Leaders recognize the importance of taking breaks. This allows employees to recharge "their batteries," redefine their focus, and maintain their positive energy levels.

9. *Learning to say no*: Leaders understand the importance of declining non-essential tasks or commitments to protect their time and resources. This skill is often difficult to grasp, yet it can be done gracefully and diplomatically.

10. *Reflecting and adjusting*: Leaders regularly review and adjust their time management strategies to ensure they maximize their productivity and achieve their goals.

Time management is an essential skill for all leaders, as it allows them to prioritize tasks, stay organized, and efficiently use their time. When leaders effectively manage their time, they are able to meet deadlines, make timely decisions, and maintain a clear focus on their goals. This not only helps them to be more productive but also sets a positive example for their team. Leaders who are able to manage their time effectively stand out by being reliable, efficient, and capable of handling multiple responsibilities without becoming overwhelmed. This ability to prioritize and stay on track can also inspire and motivate others to do the same, ultimately leading to greater success for a business as a whole.

This could further inspire you to utilize this skill in your own life. There are also many benefits of balancing time in personal situations.

Ways time management can improve everyday life:

1. *Increased productivity*: Effective time management can help you prioritize tasks and use your time more efficiently, resulting in increased productivity and accomplishment of goals.
2. *Reduced stress*: By managing your time effectively, you can reduce the stress of feeling overwhelmed by tasks and deadlines, leading to a more balanced and relaxed lifestyle.
3. *Improved focus*: Time management allows you to allocate dedicated time for specific tasks, helping you stay focused and avoid distractions. This leads to better quality work and improved concentration.
4. *Better work-life balance*: By managing your time effectively, you can create a better balance between work, personal life, and leisure activities, leading to a more fulfilling and enjoyable life.
5. *Enhanced decision-making*: Good time management can improve decision-making by allocating the right amount of time and resources to each task, leading to more thoughtful and well-planned choices.
6. *Increased motivation*: Effective time management can help you set and achieve realistic goals, which can lead to a sense

of accomplishment and increased motivation to tackle new challenges.

7. *Improved relationships*: By managing your time effectively, you can allocate time for meaningful interactions with friends and family, which can strengthen and enrich your relationships.
8. *Better health*: Effective time management allows you to allocate time for self-care, exercise, and relaxation, which can improve physical and mental well-being.
9. *Enhanced organization*: Effective time management can help you stay organized and reduce clutter, leading to a more efficient and streamlined daily life.
10. *Greater opportunities*: By managing your time effectively, you can create more personal and professional growth opportunities, which can lead to a more fulfilling and successful life.

Not everyone is gifted with the ability to apply time management effectively. For some, it may come naturally, while others feel fortunate to make it on time to each event by the seat of their pants! Fortunately, becoming an effective manager of your own time is attainable. It will take time, effort, thought, and intention, but it is a skill that can and should be learned.

Ways to develop or improve time management skills:

1. *Set clear goals*: Define your short-term and long-term goals and prioritize them according to their importance and urgency.
2. *Prioritize tasks*: Identify the most important and urgent tasks and focus on completing them first. Use techniques like the

Eisenhower Matrix, a time management tool that helps you prioritize tasks based on urgency and importance.

3. *Plan your day*: Create a daily schedule or to-do list to help you stay organized and focused. Break down larger tasks into smaller, manageable steps.

4. *Minimize distractions*: Identify and eliminate or minimize distractions that can derail your focus and productivity, such as social media, email, or unnecessary meetings.

5. *Learn to say no*: Don't overcommit yourself to tasks or activities not aligned with your goals and priorities. It's okay to decline or delegate tasks when necessary.

6. *Delegate tasks*: If possible, delegate tasks to others to free up your time for more important responsibilities.

7. *Use time management tools*: Tools such as calendars, to-do lists, and time-tracking apps can help you stay organized and manage your time effectively. Many different tools are available; research which one works best for you. Journal daily to get your thoughts on paper or digitally to clear them from your mind. This opens your mind to free-flow thinking and establishes a record of your current thoughts.

8. *Set deadlines*: Establish realistic deadlines for tasks and hold yourself accountable to meet them.

9. *Take breaks*: Incorporate short breaks into your workday to recharge and maintain focus. Avoid working long stretches without a break, as it can lead to burnout and decreased productivity.

10. *Reflect and adjust*: Regularly assess your time management strategies and make adjustments as needed. Consider what's

working well and where you can improve. Flexibility and adaptability are key to effective time management.

Time management is crucial as it helps you prioritize tasks and set realistic goals, leading to increased productivity and efficiency. It also reduces stress and becoming overwhelmed by providing structure and organization to daily activities. Effective time management allows for a better work-life balance, enabling you to allocate time for both work and personal activities. Additionally, it promotes a sense of accountability and discipline, leading to greater success and achievement in both professional and personal endeavors. Managing time effectively is crucial for maximizing productivity, reducing stress, and achieving a healthy work-life balance.

 Reflect:

1. Have you ever worked for a corrupt, manipulative, or divisive boss? How did you deal with this type of behavior? What were the results? What did you do correctly?

2. What changes will you make as a result of this chapter? What is your desired outcome?

3. Where does the toxic behavior stem from? Is it solely with your immediate boss, or is there an issue with the company's management in general? What will you do if the issue is only with your boss? What will you do if it is company-wide?

4. What are some dangers of a toxic leader? What can you do when faced with this situation? What can you add to the list provided in this chapter?

5. What do you know about integrity? How can integrity be used effectively in leadership? How can integrity be used as an employee? Describe a time when you lacked integrity in a situation. Describe a time when you exemplified integrity despite challenging circumstances. Compare and contrast each example. What do you notice?

6. Find ways to program integrity into your "preprogram." More information about how to "Reprogram Your Pre-Program" is found in *Elevate Your Mind to Success, Success Is EleMENTAL*, and at www.ABookinTime.net.

7. Describe good time management. How is this used effectively as a leader? How can it be used effectively as an employee?

8. Rate your current ability to manage time. What are you doing correctly? How can you improve?

9. What are some benefits of proper time management? How can this be applied to a situation involving a toxic boss?

10. Research more about integrity and good time management and practice these valuable skills daily.

PART 2

When Coworkers Don't "Co-Work"

CHAPTER 7
The Disengager

A disengaged employee is like a candle without a flame—he may still be present but does not provide light or warmth to those around him.

—Jill Fandrich

To "co-work" means to work alongside others in a shared space, often with people from different backgrounds or skill sets. It involves sharing resources, ideas, and collaboration to create a productive and supportive work environment. We covered many chapters regarding ineffective and even destructive leadership. Now, let's look at employee behavior and how it can affect not only the leader but also the company and other team members.

A disengaged employee lacks motivation and enthusiasm for his work, which can lead to poor performance and negatively impact team morale.

Characteristics of Disengagers:

1. *Lack of motivation*: Disengaged employees often lack the motivation to perform their duties to the best of their abilities.
2. *Low productivity*: They may have lower productivity levels and not promptly meet deadlines or complete tasks.

3. *Negative attitude*: Disengaged employees may have a negative attitude toward their work, colleagues, and the company as a whole.
4. *Lack of enthusiasm*: They may show little enthusiasm for their work and may not take pride in their accomplishments.
5. *Absenteeism*: Disengaged employees may have a higher absenteeism rate and take more sick days or time off than their engaged counterparts.
6. *Lack of initiative*: They may lack the initiative to take on new challenges or seek out opportunities for growth and development.
7. *Resistance to change*: Disengaged employees may resist change and be reluctant to adapt to new processes or procedures.
8. *Poor communication*: They may have difficulty communicating effectively with their colleagues and may not participate in team activities or meetings.
9. *Lack of commitment*: Disengaged employees may show little commitment to the company's goals and may not go above and beyond their basic job responsibilities.
10. *Disconnection from the company culture*: They may feel disconnected from the company's culture and may not align with its values and mission, which can lead to a lack of loyalty.

Disengaged employees can negatively affect the boss in several ways. Their lack of motivation and productivity can result in decreased overall team performance, impacting the boss's ability to meet goals and targets. Also, a disengaged employee may create a negative work environment, leading to decreased morale and increased turnover among other team members. This can increase the boss's workload as he must manage the consequences of the disengaged employee's behavior and find replacements. The boss may have to spend time and resources attempting to re-engage the employee, diverting attention from other important tasks. Overall, a disengaged employee can have a significant negative impact on the boss's ability to lead and manage his team effectively.

An employee who disengages can negatively affect other team members in several ways. For example, his lack of enthusiasm and motivation can affect the team's morale, leading to decreased productivity and a negative work environment. His disengagement may result in a lack of collaboration and communication, making it difficult for team members to work together effectively. This can also lead to resentment and frustration among other team members, who may feel like they are picking up the slack for The Disengager. Ultimately, a disengaged employee can have a ripple effect on the entire team, leading to decreased performance and overall job satisfaction.

Ways a leader can effectively work with The Disengager:

1. *Understand the root cause*: The leader should take the time to understand the reasons behind the employee's disengagement. This may involve having open and honest conversations with the employee to uncover any underlying issues.
2. *Listen and show empathy*: It's important for the leader to actively listen to the employee's concerns and show empathy toward his situation. This can help build trust and create a more supportive work environment.
3. *Provide support and resources*: The leader should offer support and resources to help the employee overcome his

disengagement. This may involve offering additional training, mentoring, or coaching to help the employee improve his performance and motivation.

4. *Set clear goals and expectations*: The leader should set clear and achievable goals for the employee, as well as provide regular feedback to help him stay on track. This can help the employee feel more engaged and motivated to improve performance.

5. *Offer opportunities for growth and development*: Providing opportunities for the disengaged employee to learn new skills, take on new challenges, or participate in meaningful projects can help reignite a passion for his work.

6. *Recognize and reward efforts*: Acknowledging and rewarding employees' efforts can help boost morale and motivation. This can be as simple as verbal recognition or more formal rewards such as bonuses or promotions.

7. *Create a positive work environment*: The leader should strive to create a positive and inclusive work environment that encourages open communication, collaboration, and a sense of belonging for all employees.

8. *Monitor progress and provide ongoing support*: The leader should continuously monitor the employee's progress and provide ongoing support as needed. This can help ensure that the employee remains engaged and motivated over time.

Highlighted Character Quality:

Accountability:

What is accountability, and how does it fit into leadership? Accountability is the obligation or willingness to accept responsibility for your actions, decisions, and behavior. It involves being answerable and transparent about your actions and holding yourself or others to a certain standard of conduct. In a broader sense, accountability also refers to the mechanisms and processes in place to ensure that people and organizations are held responsible for their actions and are subject to consequences for any wrongdoing.

Accountability in leadership is used to ensure that people are held responsible for their actions, decisions, and performance. It helps to create a culture of trust, transparency, and ownership within the team or organization. Leaders use accountability to set clear expectations, provide support and resources, and hold individuals accountable for their commitments and results. This can involve regular check-ins, performance evaluations, and constructive feedback to ensure everyone is aligned with the organization's goals and values. By promoting accountability, leaders can foster a sense of responsibility, motivation, and excellence within their teams.

Benefits of accountability:

1. *Increased productivity*: When held accountable for your actions and goals, you are more likely to stay focused and motivated, leading to higher productivity levels.

2. *Improved performance*: Accountability encourages you to take ownership of your work and strive for excellence, leading to improved performance and results.
3. *Enhanced trust and teamwork*: When everyone is held accountable, it creates a culture of trust and teamwork, as you can rely on each other to fulfill responsibilities and contribute to the team's overall success.
4. *Clear communication*: Accountability requires clear communication and expectations, which can help prevent misunderstandings and conflicts within a team or organization.
5. *Personal growth and development*: Being held accountable encourages you to take responsibility for your actions, learn from mistakes, and continuously improve skills and knowledge.
6. *Greater transparency and integrity*: Accountability fosters a culture of transparency and integrity, as you are expected to be honest and open about your actions and decisions.
7. *Achievement of goals*: Accountability helps you stay focused on goals and take the necessary steps to achieve them, leading to greater success and fulfillment.

Ways to develop or improve accountability:

1. *Setting clear expectations*: Clearly communicate expectations, including specific goals, timelines, and responsibilities.
2. *Establishing consequences*: Clearly outline the consequences for failing to meet expectations or not taking responsibility for your actions. This could include performance reviews, loss of privileges, or other disciplinary measures.

3. *Encouraging open communication*: Create a culture where individuals feel comfortable discussing challenges and seeking help when needed. This can help prevent issues from escalating and promote a sense of ownership and responsibility.

4. *Providing support and resources*: Ensure people have access to the necessary resources, training, and support to help them meet their responsibilities. This can include mentorship, coaching, and access to tools and technology.

5. *Leading by example*: Leaders and managers should model accountability in their own actions and decisions. This can help set a positive example for others to follow.

6. *Regular monitoring and feedback*: Regularly monitor progress toward goals and provide constructive feedback to individuals and teams. This can help identify areas for improvement and reinforce the importance of accountability.

7. *Recognizing and rewarding accountability*: Acknowledge and reward individuals and teams who demonstrate accountability and take ownership of their responsibilities. This can help reinforce positive behaviors and encourage others to do the same.

Being accountable in daily life is crucial for personal and professional growth. It is also a quality many people lack. It is that much more important to incorporate accountability into your leadership arsenal. It helps build trust and credibility with others, as people can rely on you to fulfill your commitments and responsibilities. Being accountable also fosters a sense of ownership and empowerment, as it encourages you to take control of your actions and decisions. It leads to better time management, productivity, and overall success in achieving goals. Additionally, accountability promotes integrity and ethical behavior, essential for maintaining healthy relationships and a positive reputation. Accountability is a key factor in leading a fulfilling and purposeful life, both personally and professionally.

Highlighted Leadership Skill:

Clear Vision:

What is it to set a clear vision, and how does it fit into leadership? Setting a clear vision means defining a specific and compelling goal or objective for an individual, team, or organization. It involves articulating a clear and inspiring picture of what success looks like and how it will be achieved. This vision provides direction, motivation, and a sense of purpose for everyone involved, helping to align efforts and resources toward a common destination. A clear vision also helps guide decision-making and prioritize actions in order to progress toward the desired outcome.

Setting a clear vision is essential in leadership because it provides direction and purpose for the team or organization. It helps align everyone toward a common goal, motivate and inspire them, and guide decision-making. A clear vision also helps create a sense of unity and focus and allows leaders to effectively communicate their goals and expectations to their team. Additionally, it can help gain support and commitment from colleagues and evaluate progress and success. Setting a clear vision is crucial for effective leadership and success.

Benefits of having a clear vision:

1. *Clarity:* A clear vision provides a sense of direction and purpose, helping prioritize goals and focus on what is important.

2. *Motivation*: A clear vision can inspire and motivate you to work toward a common goal, fostering a sense of commitment and dedication.

3. *Alignment:* A clear vision helps align efforts, ensuring everyone works toward the same objectives.

4. *Decision-making*: A clear vision provides a framework for decision-making, making it easier to evaluate choices and determine the best course of action.

5. *Resilience*: A clear vision can provide a sense of resilience and determination, helping to overcome challenges and setbacks.

6. *Innovation*: A clear vision can stimulate creativity and innovation, encouraging you to think outside the box and explore new possibilities.

7. *Accountability:* A clear vision holds you accountable for your actions, provides a benchmark for success, and aids in measuring progress.

8. *Communication*: A clear vision provides a common language and understanding, facilitating effective communication and collaboration.

9. *Satisfaction*: A clear vision can lead to a sense of fulfillment and satisfaction as you work toward achieving your goals.

10. *Success:* Ultimately, a clear vision can lead to success, as it provides a roadmap for achieving desired outcomes and realizing potential.

Ways to improve your vision-setting skills:

1. *Define the purpose*: Clearly state the purpose and objectives of the vision, ensuring that everyone understands and is aligned with the overall goal.
2. *Communicate effectively*: Clearly communicate the vision to all colleagues and ensure they understand the importance and benefits of achieving it.
3. *Involve stakeholders*: Involve key stakeholders or colleagues in the process of setting the vision to ensure that their perspectives and input are considered.
4. Create a roadmap: Develop a clear and actionable roadmap for achieving the vision, including specific milestones and timelines.
5. *Lead by example*: Demonstrate commitment and passion for the vision, inspiring others also to be committed and motivated.
6. *Monitor progress*: Regularly monitor and evaluate progress toward the vision, making adjustments as necessary to stay on track.
7. *Provide support and resources*: Ensure that the necessary support and resources are in place in order to achieve the vision.
8. *Foster a positive culture*: Create a positive, inclusive culture that aligns with the vision and encourages collaboration and innovation.
9. *Celebrate achievements*: Recognize and celebrate milestones and achievements along the way. This will reinforce the importance of the vision and motivate others to continue working toward it.

10. *Adapt and evolve*: Be open to feedback and willing to alter and update the vision as needed to ensure it remains relevant and achievable.

A clear vision in daily life is essential because it provides direction and purpose. It allows you to set goals and work toward achieving them, making it easier to make decisions and prioritize tasks. A clear vision also helps you stay focused, motivated, and resilient in the face of challenges and obstacles. It can also create a sense of fulfillment and satisfaction as progress is made toward the desired outcome. Also, a clear vision can inspire and motivate others, leading to greater collaboration and success in both personal and professional endeavors.

 Reflect:

1. Have you ever worked with a Disengager? How did you deal with this type of behavior? What were the results? What did you do correctly?
2. What changes will you make as a result of this chapter? What is your desired outcome?
3. What are the challenges involved with a Disengager? How do they affect the work environment? Are they solely with one employee or with more than one? What will you do if the issue is with one employee? What will you do if it is widespread?
4. What are some dangers of a disengaged employee? What can you do when faced with this situation? What can you add to the list provided in this chapter?
5. What do you know about accountability? How can accountability be used effectively in your personal and professional life?

Describe a time when you lacked accountability in a situation. Describe a time when you displayed accountability despite challenging circumstances. Compare and contrast each example. What do you notice?

6. Find ways to program accountability into your "preprogram." More information about how to "Reprogram Your Pre-Program" is found in *Elevate Your Mind to Success, Success Is Ele-MENTAL*, and at www.ABookinTime.net.

7. Describe a clear vision. How is this used effectively as a leader? How can it be used effectively in daily life?

8. Rate your current ability to develop a clear vision in your professional life. Rate your current ability to develop a clear vision in your personal life. What are you doing correctly? How can you improve?

9. What are some benefits of establishing a clear vision? How can this be applied to a situation involving a disengaged employee?

10. Research more about accountability and a clear vision and practice these valuable skills daily.

CHAPTER 8
The Procrastinator

A procrastinating employee is like a thief of time, stealing productivity, progress, and success in the workplace.

—Jill Fandrich

A procrastinating employee consistently puts off or delays completing work tasks, often resulting in missed deadlines and lower productivity. This behavior can result from poor time management, lack of motivation, or feeling overwhelmed by the workload. Procrastinators can negatively impact a team or organization's overall performance and efficiency.

Characteristics of Procrastinators:

1. *Delays in completing tasks*: Procrastinating employees often put off completing tasks until the last minute, which can result in missed deadlines and poor-quality work.
2. *Lack of time management skills*: Procrastinators may struggle with managing their time effectively, leading to a backlog of work and increased stress.
3. *Difficulty prioritizing tasks*: Procrastinators may have trouble prioritizing tasks and may focus on less important activities instead of urgent or high-impact tasks.

4. *Tendency to avoid difficult tasks*: Procrastinators may avoid tackling difficult or challenging tasks, opting instead for easier, less demanding work.

5. *Increased stress and anxiety*: Procrastinators may experience increased stress and anxiety as deadlines approach and work continues to pile up.

6. *Inconsistent work habits*: Procrastinators may exhibit inconsistent work habits, alternating between intense productivity and inactivity periods.

7. *Unfavorable impact on team dynamics*: Procrastinating employees may negatively impact team dynamics by causing delays in collaborative projects and creating frustration among their colleagues.

8. *Difficulty with self-discipline*: Procrastinators may struggle with self-discipline and require additional support and accountability to stay on track with their work.

Procrastinating employees can negatively affect the boss in several ways. Their delay in completing tasks can lead to missed deadlines, which can impact the overall productivity and success of the team or company. This can also create a bottleneck effect, causing other team members to have to pick up the slack or causing a domino effect of delays. Procrastinators can also create a negative work environment by causing frustration and stress for their colleagues and the boss. This can lead to decreased morale and motivation, as well as strained relationships within the team.

Furthermore, the boss may be forced to spend more time and effort managing and monitoring Procrastinators, which can reduce his ability to focus on other important tasks and responsibilities. If these employees are allowed to get away with their behavior, this can also create a perception of favoritism or unfairness. Is it any wonder procrastinating employees can have a significantly negative impact on the boss, the team, and the organization's overall success?

Procrastination by an employee can negatively affect the staff in several ways. It can lead to missed deadlines and increased workloads for other team members, causing resentment and frustration. It can also create a lack of trust and reliability within the team, as others may have to pick up the slack for the Procrastinator. This can lead to a decrease in overall productivity and morale within the team. Procrastination can also impact the quality of work produced, as rushed or last-minute efforts may not meet the necessary standards. A Procrastinator can create a ripple effect of negative consequences for the entire staff.

Ways a leader can work with Procrastinators:

1. *Understand the root cause*: Take the time to understand why employees procrastinate. It could be due to a lack of clarity, fear of failure, or feeling overwhelmed. Understanding the underlying reason will help in finding a solution.
2. *Set clear expectations*: Clearly communicate the tasks' expectations and deadlines. Ensure the employees understand the importance of the work and the consequences of not completing it on time.
3. *Provide support and resources*: Offer support and resources to help the employees overcome procrastination. This could include training, mentoring, or additional tools to help them manage their time and tasks more effectively.

4. *Break tasks into smaller steps*: Help the employees break down their tasks into smaller, manageable steps. This can make the work seem less daunting and help them get started.

5. *Hold them accountable*: Check in regularly to monitor progress and hold the employees accountable for their work. This will help them stay on track and provide an opportunity for support or feedback if needed.

6. *Offer incentives*: Consider offering rewards or incentives for meeting deadlines and completing tasks on time. Positive reinforcement can motivate employees to overcome procrastination. This doesn't need to be extravagant. Sometimes, the smallest incentive will be enough to show employees that you care about them and their work.

7. *Encourage open communication*: Create a safe and open environment where employees feel comfortable discussing their challenges and seeking help. Encouraging open communication can help identify and address any underlying issues contributing to procrastination.

Highlighted Character Quality:

Initiative:

What is initiative, and how does it fit into leadership? Initiative is taking charge and acting independently to accomplish a task or goal. It involves being proactive, innovative, and willing to take the lead in a given situation. Having initiative means identifying and pursuing opportunities, making decisions, and taking action without being told or directed by others. It is an important quality in personal and professional development, as it demonstrates drive, ambition, and a willingness to go above and beyond what is expected.

Initiative is the ability to take action and make decisions without being prompted or directed. In leadership, initiative drives progress, solves problems, and achieves goals. A leader who takes initiative demonstrates proactivity, decisiveness, and a willingness to take risks. By taking initiative, a leader can inspire and motivate others, set a positive example, and drive positive organizational change. Initiative in leadership involves recognizing opportunities, making decisions, and taking action to move the organization forward. It also requires a willingness to take on new challenges and responsibilities and to lead by example. Initiative is critical for effective leadership, enabling leaders to drive innovation, adapt to change, and achieve success.

Benefits of initiative:

1. *Increased productivity*: Taking initiative and being proactive can lead to more efficient work processes and higher productivity levels.
2. *Personal growth*: By taking initiative, you can develop new skills, expand your knowledge, and gain confidence in your abilities.
3. *Career advancement*: When you demonstrate initiative, you are often seen as a valuable asset to your organization and are more likely to be considered for promotions or new opportunities.
4. *Problem-solving*: Taking initiative involves identifying and addressing challenges or opportunities, which can lead to innovative solutions and organizational improvements.

5. *Leadership development*: Initiative is a key characteristic of influential leaders, and taking initiative can help you develop your leadership skills and qualities.
6. *Positive reputation*: When you take initiative, you are often seen as proactive, responsible, and reliable, which can enhance your reputation within your organization and industry.
7. *Increased autonomy*: Taking initiative can lead to greater independence and autonomy in your work, allowing you to take ownership of your responsibilities and make more confident decisions.
8. *Adaptability:* Initiative fosters a mindset of adaptability and flexibility, enabling you to respond to changes and challenges with creativity and resourcefulness.
9. *Enhanced teamwork*: When you take initiative, you can inspire and motivate your colleagues, leading to a more proactive and collaborative work environment.
10. *Personal satisfaction*: Taking initiative and achieving successful outcomes can lead to a sense of fulfillment and pride in your work.

Ways to develop or improve initiative:

1. *Set clear goals for yourself*: Having a clear idea of what you want to achieve will help you take the initiative to work toward those goals.
2. *Take on new challenges*: Stepping out of your comfort zone and taking on new challenges can help you develop your initiative and problem-solving skills.

3. *Be proactive*: Instead of waiting for opportunities to come to you, seek them out and take the initiative to make things happen.
4. *Practice decision-making*: Making decisions and taking responsibility for the outcomes can help you develop your initiative and confidence in your abilities.
5. *Seek feedback*: Asking for feedback from others can help you identify areas for improvement and learn from your experiences.
6. *Learn from failure*: Don't be afraid to take risks and learn from your failures. Failure can be a great informational tool and help you develop your initiative and resilience.
7. *Cultivate a growth mindset*: Embrace challenges and see them as opportunities for growth and development.
8. *Take ownership of your work*: Instead of waiting for instructions, take ownership of your work and look for ways to improve processes and outcomes.
9. *Network and collaborate*: Building relationships with others can provide opportunities for collaboration and new initiatives.
10. *Stay motivated*: Keep yourself motivated by setting small, achievable goals and celebrating your successes. Enjoy the process of advancing to bigger goals as you achieve smaller ones. Challenge yourself and enjoy the journey.

Taking initiative in daily life is important because it allows you to take control of your own life, make things happen, and create opportunities for yourself. It helps to develop a proactive mindset, increase productivity, and drive personal and professional growth. Taking initiative also leads to greater self-confidence, independence, and the ability to embrace new challenges. It can also inspire and motivate you, create positive change, and contribute to overall success and fulfillment in life. Ultimately, taking initiative enables you to live with purpose and achieve your goals.

Highlighted Leadership Skill:

Team Development:

What is team development, and how does it fit into leadership? Team development is the process of building and improving the performance and effectiveness of a team. It involves various activities and strategies to enhance team members' communication, collaboration, trust, and cohesion. Team development also focuses on identifying and leveraging the strengths of each team member, as well as addressing any conflicts or challenges that may arise within the team. Team development aims to create a high-performing and cohesive team to achieve its goals and objectives more effectively.

Team development is a crucial aspect of leadership as it involves improving the performance and cohesion of a group of individuals working toward a common goal. Leaders use team development to build trust, communication, and collaboration among team members, ultimately leading to higher productivity and efficiency. This process involves various strategies such as team building activities, conflict resolution, skill development, and regular feedback to ensure the team works together effectively. Effective team development also helps identify and utilize the strengths of each team member, create a positive work environment, and foster a sense of belonging and commitment among team members. Team development is a key tool for leaders to create a strong and successful team.

Benefits of team development:

1. *Improved communication*: Team development activities can help team members develop better communication skills, leading to more effective and efficient collaboration.
2. *Increased trust and cohesion*: Team development activities can build trust and strengthen the relationships between team members, leading to a more cohesive and supportive team environment.
3. *Enhanced problem-solving skills*: Team development activities can help team members develop problem-solving skills and learn to work together to overcome challenges and obstacles.
4. *Improved productivity*: When team members are able to work together more effectively and communicate more efficiently, productivity is likely to increase.
5. *Better conflict resolution*: Team development activities can help team members learn to manage and resolve conflicts constructively and respectfully.
6. *Greater creativity and innovation*: A well-developed team is more likely to generate new ideas and innovative solutions, leading to a more competitive and successful team.
7. *Increased job satisfaction*: When team members feel supported and valued within their team, job satisfaction is likely to improve, leading to higher levels of motivation and commitment.
8. *Better retention rates*: A strong and well-developed team is more likely to retain its members, reducing turnover and the associated costs of recruiting and training new employees.

Ways to develop or improve team development:

1. *Clear communication*: Encourage open and transparent communication within the team to ensure everyone is on the same page and can share ideas and concerns freely.
2. *Set clear goals and expectations*: Clearly define the team's goals and the individual roles and responsibilities of each team member. This will help everyone understand what is expected of them and how their work contributes to the overall team objectives.
3. *Foster a positive team culture*: Create a supportive and collaborative environment where team members feel valued and respected. Encourage teamwork and mutual support to build a cohesive and motivated team.
4. *Provide opportunities for skill development*: Offer training and development opportunities for team members to enhance their skills and knowledge, which can improve their performance and contribute to the team's success.
5. *Encourage feedback and recognition*: Regularly provide feedback to team members on their performance and recognize their contributions to the team. This will help boost morale and motivation and also provide opportunities for improvement.
6. *Promote teamwork and collaboration*: Encourage team members to work together and collaborate on projects. This will help build trust and strengthen their relationships, leading to a more cohesive and effective team.
7. *Foster a sense of ownership*: Encourage team members to take ownership of their work and contribute to the decision-making process. This will help them feel more invested in the team's success and take more responsibility for their work.

8. *Foster diversity*: Embrace diversity in the team and create an inclusive environment where everyone feels valued and respected. This will help bring different perspectives and ideas to the table, leading to more innovative solutions and better team performance.
9. *Provide resources and support*: Ensure the team has the necessary resources and support to work effectively. This can include providing the right tools, equipment, and support from management.
10. *Lead by example*: As a leader, set a positive example for the team by demonstrating good communication, teamwork, and a strong work ethic. This will inspire team members to follow suit and contribute to the overall development of the team.

Team development is an important skill as it helps to build trust and collaboration among team members, leading to improved communication and a more positive work environment. It can also lead to increased productivity and efficiency as team members learn to work together more effectively. Team development also helps identify and develop individual team member's strengths, leading to a more well-rounded and high-performing team. Ultimately, team development is essential for creating a cohesive and well-developed unit to achieve its goals and contribute to overall success.

 Reflect:

1. Have you ever worked with a Procrastinator? How did you deal with this type of behavior? What were the results? What did you do correctly?

2. What changes will you make as a result of this chapter? What is your desired outcome?

3. What are the challenges involved with a Procrastinator? How do they affect the work environment? Are they solely with one employee or with more than one? What will you do if the issue is with one employee? What will you do if it is widespread?

4. What are some dangers of a procrastinating employee? What can you do when faced with this situation? What can you add to the list provided in this chapter?

5. What do you know about initiative? How can taking initiative be used effectively in your personal and professional life? Describe a time when you lacked initiative in a situation. Describe a time when you showed initiative despite challenging circumstances. Compare and contrast each example. What do you notice?

6. Find ways to program initiative into your "preprogram." More information about how to "Reprogram Your Pre-Program" is found in *Elevate Your Mind to Success, Success Is EleMENTAL*, and at www.ABookinTime.net.

7. Describe team development. How is this used effectively as a leader? How can it be used effectively in daily life?

8. Rate your current ability to develop a team in your professional life. Rate your current ability to develop a team in your personal life, such as your family. What are you doing correctly? How can you improve?

9. What are some benefits of team development? How can this be applied to a situation involving a procrastinating employee?

10. Research more about initiative and team development and practice these valuable skills daily.

CHAPTER 9
The Micromanager

Micromanaging employees are like helicopter parents — they hover over every detail and never let go, inhibiting the growth and independence of their peers.

—Jill Fandrich

Micromanaging employees are people who closely supervise and control the work of their subordinates or coworkers, often to an excessive and unnecessary degree. They may constantly check in on them, give overly detailed instructions, and resist delegating tasks, which can lead to decreased morale and productivity among the team. Micromanagers may also struggle to trust team members to complete tasks independently, leading to inefficiency and frustration among team members.

Characteristics of Micromanagers:

1. Constantly checking in on coworkers and their work progress.
2. Difficulty delegating tasks and trusting others to complete them.
3. Needing to be involved in every decision and detail, no matter how small.
4. Overwhelming peers with unnecessary supervision and oversight.

5. Obsessing over minor details and making frequent changes to work already completed.
6. Struggling to prioritize tasks and constantly changing priorities.
7. Difficulty giving others autonomy and independence in their work.
8. Having a lack of trust in the abilities and judgment of other team members.
9. Being overly critical and nitpicky about minor mistakes.
10. Creating a tense and stressful work environment for others due to their controlling behavior.

A micromanaging employee can negatively affect the boss in several ways. The boss may feel frustrated and overwhelmed by the constant need to supervise and correct the employee's work, leading to increased stress and decreased productivity. The boss may also feel like his authority and decision-making abilities are being undermined, which can lead to a strained working relationship. Micromanaging employees can also create a toxic and demotivating work environment, as other employees may feel undervalued and disempowered. Micromanagers can ultimately hinder the boss's ability to effectively lead and manage his team, leading to decreased overall performance and success.

Micromanaging employees can lead to a loss of autonomy and decision-making power for coworkers, resulting in decreased job satisfaction and motivation. They can also create a tense and stressful work environment, as coworkers may feel constantly scrutinized and criticized. This can lead to decreased productivity and creativity, as employees may hesitate to take risks or implement new ideas. Furthermore, Micromanagers can damage coworker relationships, as they can breed resentment and a lack of trust. The negative effects of micromanagement can lead other employees to decreased job satisfaction, increased stress, and reduced overall productivity for the entire team.

Ways a leader can work with Micromanagers:

1. *Set clear expectations*: Clearly communicate the project or task's goals and objectives and provide detailed instructions on how the work should be done. This can help alleviate employees' micromanaging tendencies by giving them a clear roadmap to follow.
2. *Provide regular feedback*: Offer constructive feedback on the employees' work, highlighting both their strengths and areas for improvement. This can help build the employees' confidence and reduce the need for constant oversight.
3. *Empower the employee*: Encourage them to take ownership of their work and make decisions independently. Giving them the autonomy to solve problems and make choices can help reduce their need for micromanaging.
4. *Communicate openly*: Have open and honest conversations with employees about their tendency to micromanage. Express your trust in their abilities and reassure them that you are there to support them.
5. *Delegate effectively*: Assign tasks and responsibilities to employees based on their strengths and capabilities. This can help them feel more empowered and reduce their need to micromanage.
6. *Lead by example*: Demonstrate trust and confidence in the employees' abilities by allowing them to take the lead on

certain projects. Show them that you trust their judgment and decision-making skills.

7. *Provide resources and support*: Offer employees the resources and support they need to succeed in their roles. This can help build their confidence and reduce their reliance on micromanaging.

8. *Create a positive work environment*: Foster a positive and supportive work environment where employees feel valued and appreciated. This can help reduce the need for micromanaging as employees feel more motivated and empowered to take ownership of their work.

9. *Emphasize team unity*: Let it be known that you work in a team environment where everyone is valued and responsible to participate effectively and respectfully with others.

Highlighted Character Quality:

Adaptability:

What is adaptability, and how does it fit into leadership? Adaptability is the ability to adjust to new conditions, environments, or situations. It involves being flexible, open-minded, and able to respond effectively to change. Adaptable people are able to thrive in different circumstances and can quickly learn and adjust to new challenges. Adaptability is an important skill in personal, professional, and social contexts.

Adaptability in leadership refers to the ability of leaders to adjust to new circumstances, challenges, and changes in the environment. It involves being flexible, open-minded, and able to think on their feet. Adaptability in leadership is used to effectively navigate and lead through uncertain and volatile situations, to quickly adjust strategies and plans as needed, and to inspire and motivate others to embrace change. Adaptable leaders can guide their teams through transitions, foster innovation, and effectively respond to unexpected events. By being adaptable, leaders can create a resilient and agile organization that can thrive in a rapidly changing world.

Benefits of adaptability:

1. *Increased resilience*: Being adaptable allows you to bounce back from challenges and setbacks more easily, making you more resilient in the face of adversity.
2. *Improved problem-solving skills*: When adaptable, you are more adept at finding creative and effective solutions to problems and can think "on your feet" when presented with unexpected challenges.
3. *Enhanced job performance*: Adaptability in the workplace can lead to improved performance, allowing you to quickly adjust to changing circumstances, learn new skills, and take on new responsibilities.
4. *Better interpersonal relationships*: Being adaptable means being more open to new ideas and perspectives, strengthening relationships, and improving collaboration with others.
5. *Increased career opportunities*: Employers value adaptability and are more likely to promote and reward you as you can quickly adapt to new situations and environments.
6. *Greater personal growth*: When adaptable, you are more open to new experiences and are constantly learning and growing, leading to personal development and self-improvement.

7. *Reduced stress*: The ability to adapt to change can lead to decreased stress and anxiety, as you are better equipped to handle unexpected situations and uncertainties.
8. *Enhanced decision-making*: When adaptable, you are able to make quick and effective decisions in the face of uncertainty, leading to better outcomes and results.

Ways to improve or become more adaptable:

1. *Embrace change*: Accept that change is a natural part of life and be open to new experiences and challenges.
2. *Develop a growth mindset*: Cultivate a positive attitude toward learning and see challenges as opportunities for personal growth.
3. *Practice mindfulness*: Learn to be present in the moment and be aware of your thoughts and emotions. This can help you better cope with change and adapt to new situations.
4. *Be open-minded*: Try to see things from different perspectives and be willing to consider new ideas and approaches.
5. *Build resilience*: Develop the ability to bounce back from setbacks and learn from difficult experiences.
6. *Develop new skills*: Continuously seek to learn new skills and expand your knowledge, which can help you adapt to different situations and environments.
7. *Seek feedback*: Be open to receiving feedback from others and use it as an opportunity to learn and grow.
8. *Be proactive*: Take initiative and be proactive in seeking out new opportunities and experiences.

9. *Cultivate a support network*: Surround yourself with people who can support and guide you during times of change and uncertainty.

10. *Practice self-care*: Take care of your physical and mental well-being, as this can help you better cope with stress and adapt to change.

11. *Read more*: Read or listen to books, articles, strategies, or new methods or ways of doing things. Seek to constantly increase your knowledge.

Becoming more adaptable is essential in today's rapidly changing world because it allows you to respond effectively to new challenges and opportunities. Adaptable people are better able to learn new skills, adjust to changing circumstances, and thrive in diverse and dynamic environments. This flexibility and resilience are key traits for success in both personal and professional realms, as they enable you to navigate uncertainty, embrace innovation, and remain competitive in an evolving global landscape. Being more adaptable can lead to greater personal growth, improved problem-solving abilities, and increased overall satisfaction and success.

Highlighted Leadership Skill:

Conflict Resolution:

What is conflict resolution, and how does it fit into leadership? Conflict resolution is the process of addressing and resolving disputes, disagreements, or conflicts between individuals or groups constructively and peacefully. It involves identifying the underlying issues, communicating effectively, and finding a mutually acceptable resolution. Conflict resolution can be achieved through various methods such as negotiation, mediation, arbitration, or compromise. It aims to promote understanding, cooperation, and positive relationships among those involved in the conflict.

Conflict resolution is a crucial skill for effective leadership. In leadership, it is used to address and manage conflicts that arise between team members, departments, or other colleagues. It involves identifying the root cause of the conflict, facilitating open communication, and finding a mutually satisfactory solution. Leaders use conflict resolution to promote a positive and productive work environment, build trust among team members, and drive collaboration and innovation. By effectively resolving conflicts, leaders can prevent negative impacts on team morale, productivity, and overall success. Conflict resolution also allows leaders to model effective communication and problem-solving skills, which can positively influence their team and organizational culture.

Benefits of conflict resolution:

1. *Improved relationships*: Conflict resolution can help improve relationships by addressing underlying issues and finding mutually acceptable solutions.
2. *Increased productivity*: Resolving conflicts can lead to increased productivity, as it eliminates distractions and allows you to focus on your work.
3. *Better communication*: Conflict resolution can improve communication by encouraging you to express your concerns and listen to each other's perspectives.
4. *Reduced stress*: Addressing and resolving conflicts can reduce stress and tension in the workplace, leading to a more positive and harmonious environment.

5. *Enhanced problem-solving skills*: Conflict resolution requires you to think critically and creatively to find solutions, which can improve your problem-solving skills.
6. *Increased trust and respect*: Resolving conflicts fairly and respectfully can help build trust and respect among team members.
7. *Improved collaboration*: Effective conflict resolution can promote collaboration and teamwork as you work together to find solutions and reach common goals.
8. *Better decision-making*: Resolving conflicts can lead to better decision-making by encouraging you to consider different perspectives and weigh the pros and cons of various solutions.
9. *Greater job satisfaction*: Addressing and resolving conflicts can lead to greater job satisfaction as you feel heard and valued in the workplace.
10. *Reduced turnover*: Conflict resolution can help reduce turnover by addressing issues that may lead to employees leaving the organization.

Ways to develop or improve conflict resolution skills:

1. *Communicate effectively*: Use clear and respectful language to express your thoughts and feelings, and actively listen to the other person's perspective.
2. *Stay calm*: Practice mindfulness and deep breathing techniques to help manage your emotions and stay calm during conflicts.
3. *Seek understanding*: Try to understand the other person's perspective and the underlying reasons for their behavior.

4. *Find common ground*: Look for areas of agreement and focus on finding a solution that benefits both parties.
5. *Use "I" statements*: Express your feelings and needs using "I" statements to avoid blaming others and taking responsibility for your emotions.
6. *Practice empathy*: Put yourself in the other person's shoes and try to see the situation from their perspective.
7. *Collaborate*: Work with the other person to find a mutually beneficial solution.
8. *Be open to compromise*: Be willing to find a middle ground and make concessions to reach a resolution.
9. *Manage your body language*: Pay attention to your nonverbal cues and maintain open and welcoming body language.
10. *Seek feedback*: Ask for feedback from others on your conflict resolution skills and be open to learning and improving.
11. *Identify your goals*: What is more important to you—being right or preserving a friendship? Identify your priorities. Use critical thinking and evaluate the situation objectively. What if you cordially agreed to disagree? What is your desired outcome? Sometimes, it may be best to keep the peace and allow the other person to believe he is correct. Weigh the pros and cons in each circumstance.

Conflict resolution is important for several reasons. It helps maintain healthy personal and professional relationships by addressing and resolving issues before they escalate. Effective conflict resolution can also improve communication and understanding between parties, leading to better cooperation and collaboration. In a workplace setting, it can increase productivity and morale and reduce the negative impact of conflict on the organization. Additionally, conflict-resolving skills are essential for leaders and managers to effectively manage their teams and create a positive work environment. Resolving conflicts effectively is crucial for promoting peace, understanding, and positive interactions in all areas of life.

Reflect:

1. Have you ever worked with a Micromanager? How did you deal with this type of behavior? What were the results? What did you do correctly?

2. What changes will you make as a result of this chapter? What is your desired outcome?

3. What are the challenges involved with a Micromanager? How do they affect the work environment? Are they solely with one employee or with more than one? What will you do if the issue is with one employee? What will you do if it is widespread?

4. What are some dangers of a micromanaging employee? What can you do when faced with this situation? What can you add to the list provided in this chapter?

5. What do you know about adaptability? How can being adaptable be used effectively in your personal and professional life? Describe a time when you lacked adaptability in a situation. Describe a time when you displayed adaptability despite challenging circumstances. Compare and contrast each example. What do you notice?

6. Find ways to program adaptability into your "preprogram." More information about how to "Reprogram Your Pre-Program"

is found in *Elevate Your Mind to Success, Success Is Ele-MENTAL,* and at www.ABookinTime.net.

7. Describe conflict resolution. How is this used effectively as a leader? How can it be used effectively in daily life?

8. Rate your current ability to resolve conflicts in your professional life. Rate your current ability to resolve conflicts in your personal life, such as in your own family. What are you doing correctly? How can you improve?

9. What are some benefits of resolving conflicts? How can this be applied to a situation involving a micromanaging employee?

10. Research more about adaptability and conflict resolution and practice these valuable skills daily.

CHAPTER 10
The Complainer

A complaining employee is like a flat tire—you can't go anywhere until you change it.

—Jill Fandrich

Complaining employees are workers who frequently express dissatisfaction or criticism about their jobs, working conditions, or the company they work for. They may vocalize their grievances to their colleagues, managers, or the human resources department, and their complaints can range from minor issues to more serious grievances. These employees consistently focus on the negative aspects of their work and the company, spreading negativity and creating a toxic work environment.

Characteristics of Complainers:

1. *Negative attitude*: Complaining employees tend to have a consistently negative outlook on their work, their colleagues, and the company as a whole.
2. *Lack of accountability*: They often blame others or external factors for their dissatisfaction rather than taking responsibility for their own actions and attitudes.

3. *Unwillingness to problem-solve*: Instead of actively seeking solutions to their grievances, complaining employees tend to focus on the problems rather than the potential resolutions.
4. *Low morale*: Complaining employees may exhibit signs of low morale, such as disengagement, lack of motivation, and decreased productivity.
5. *Resistance to change*: They may resist change and vocally express discomfort with new processes, policies, or procedures.
6. *Pessimism*: Complaining employees may express a general sense of pessimism about the company's future or their own career prospects.
7. *Lack of teamwork*: They may have difficulty working collaboratively with others and may be perceived as negatively influencing team dynamics.
8. *Constant dissatisfaction*: Complainers often express dissatisfaction with their work, their compensation, or their working conditions on a regular basis.
9. *Disengagement:* They may appear disengaged from their work, lack enthusiasm, and show signs of burnout.
10. *Frequent grievances*: Complaining employees may frequently raise grievances, complaints, or concerns with their managers or HR department. This type of person is often "most content" when complaining.

A complaining employee can negatively affect the boss in several ways. Constant complaints can lower the team's morale and create a negative work environment, which in turn can affect productivity and overall performance. A Complainer can create tension and conflict within the team, leading to decreased collaboration and communication. Furthermore, the boss may feel overwhelmed and stressed by constantly dealing with the employee's complaints, leading to increased pressure and decreased job satisfaction. A complaining employee can have a detrimental effect on the boss and the overall work environment.

Complainers can negatively impact coworkers in several ways. Their constant complaining can create a toxic and negative work environment, which can lower morale and productivity among their colleagues. Their complaints can also create tension and conflict among team members, leading to a breakdown in communication and collaboration. This can ultimately hinder the overall success of the team and the organization. Complainers can also drain the energy and motivation of their coworkers, making it difficult for them to stay focused and engaged in their work. Sadly, a complaining employee can have a detrimental effect on the overall well-being and performance of their coworkers.

Ways a leader can effectively work with Complainers:

1. *Listen actively*: A leader should listen to the employees' complaints with an open mind and without interrupting. This shows them that their concerns are being taken seriously.
2. *Acknowledge the complaint*: It's important for a leader to acknowledge the employees' complaints and validate their feelings. This can help them feel heard and understood.
3. *Identify the root cause*: A leader should work with the Complainer to identify the underlying issue behind the complaint. This can help address the problem at its core rather than just dealing with the symptoms.
4. *Offer support*: A leader should offer support and guidance to the employees in finding a solution to their complaints. This

can include offering resources, training, or mentoring to help the employees overcome the issues.

5. *Set clear expectations*: A leader should communicate clear expectations regarding employees' behavior and performance. This can help prevent future complaints and ensure that employees understand what is expected of them.

6. *Provide constructive feedback*: A leader should provide constructive feedback to the employees on improving or addressing the issue that led to the complaint. This can help them see a path forward and feel empowered to make positive changes.

7. *Follow-up*: A leader should follow up with the complaining employees to ensure the issue has been resolved and provide ongoing support if needed. This shows them their concerns are being taken seriously and that the leader is committed to addressing them.

8. *Mindful awareness*: Be aware of the Complainer's specific complaint and ensure it is realistic. If the complaining doesn't cease, get HR involved or create another action plan for this employee. There must be an end and resolution to the complaint(s). If the issue continues, it will deplete the morale and unity of the staff, among other negative consequences.

Highlighted Character Quality:

Patience:

What is patience, and how does it fit into leadership? Patience is the ability to remain calm and tolerant in the face of delay, adversity, or frustration. It involves being able to wait calmly for something to happen or for someone to do something without becoming annoyed or agitated. Patience is a valuable quality that can help you navigate challenging situations and maintain a positive attitude.

Patience is effectively used in leadership by allowing leaders to listen to and understand their team members' perspectives, giving them the space and time to express their thoughts and feelings. This patience also helps leaders make well-thought-out decisions rather than rush into choices that could have negative consequences. It allows leaders to remain calm and composed in the face of challenges, which can inspire confidence in their team and help to maintain a positive work environment. Patience enables leaders to build trust and rapport with their team members, as they are able to demonstrate empathy and understanding, which ultimately leads to more effective and successful leadership.

Benefits of patience:

1. *Reduced stress:* Patience helps reduce stress levels by allowing you to remain calm and composed in difficult situations.
2. *Improved relationships:* Being patient with others can help to strengthen relationships and build trust. It shows that you care and are willing to listen and understand.
3. *Better decision-making:* Patience allows you to take the time to weigh your options and consider all possibilities before making a decision. This can lead to better outcomes and fewer regrets.
4. *Increased self-control:* Patience helps to develop self-control and discipline, which can be beneficial in all areas of life, from managing finances to maintaining a healthy lifestyle.

5. *Enhanced mental health:* Patience has been linked to improved mental well-being. It can help reduce anxiety, increase resilience, and promote a positive outlook on life.
6. *Greater productivity:* Patience can help you stay focused and motivated, even when faced with setbacks or delays. This can lead to increased productivity and success in achieving your goals.
7. *Improved communication:* Patience allows you to listen attentively and respond thoughtfully, leading to better communication and understanding in both personal and professional relationships.
8. *Increased respect:* When you remain calm and collected in challenging situations, you will gain increased respect and credibility from others. Being patient shows great strength and accountability for a logical response.

Ways to develop or improve patience:

1. Practice mindfulness and meditation to become more present and aware of your thoughts and reactions.
2. Identify triggers that cause impatience and work on managing them, whether through deep breathing, positive self-talk, or taking a break.
3. Set realistic expectations and be flexible when things don't go as planned.
4. Practice empathy and try to understand the perspective of others, which can help you become more patient in challenging situations.

5. Engage in activities that require patience, such as puzzles, gardening, or learning a new skill.

6. Take care of your physical health through regular exercise, proper nutrition, adequate sleep, and boosting your body's natural immunity. Enjoy detox baths to remove undesirable toxins from your body. This can help you manage stress and become more patient.

7. Seek support from friends, family, or a therapist to work through any underlying issues contributing to impatience.

8. Learn to let go of control and accept that some things are beyond your influence.

9. Practice gratitude and focus on the positive aspects of a situation rather than getting caught up in frustration.

10. Keep a journal to track your progress and reflect on instances where you handled situations with patience.

Becoming more patient is important for several reasons. Patience allows you to handle stress and difficult situations better, leading to improved mental and emotional well-being. It also fosters better relationships and communication, enabling you to listen and understand others more effectively. Furthermore, patience is essential for achieving long-term goals and success, as it encourages persistence and resilience in facing obstacles. Developing patience is crucial for personal growth, happiness, and success in various aspects of life.

Highlighted Leadership Skill:

Decisiveness:

What is decisiveness, and how does it fit into leadership? Decisiveness is the ability to make firm and quick decisions without hesitation or doubt. It involves taking action confidently and effectively in a timely manner. Decisive individuals are able to assess situations, weigh options, and choose a course of action assuredly. They are able to make decisions even in uncertain or high-pressure situations.

Decisiveness is a crucial aspect of effective leadership as it involves making timely and effective decisions in order to achieve organizational goals and objectives. A decisive leader is able to quickly assess situations, consider all available information, and make a clear and confident decision. This helps to instill trust and confidence in his team, as well as maintain momentum and drive progress within the organization. Decisive leaders can navigate through uncertainty and ambiguity, showing resilience and determination in the face of challenges. They are able to communicate their decisions effectively to their team, providing clarity and direction and inspiring others to follow their lead. Successful leaders' decisiveness is a key trait, enabling them to take decisive action, make tough decisions, and drive their teams toward success.

Benefits of decisiveness:

1. *Increased productivity:* Decisiveness allows you to make quick and effective decisions, leading to more efficient workflow and higher productivity levels.

2. *Improved time management:* Being decisive allows you to make decisions promptly, preventing delays and allowing for better time management.

3. *Enhanced problem-solving skills:* When decisive, you are better equipped to evaluate situations and devise effective solutions, leading to improved problem-solving skills.

4. *Increased confidence:* Making decisions confidently can boost self-esteem and confidence, leading to a more positive outlook and improved overall well-being.

5. *Better leadership skills:* Decisiveness is a crucial trait of influential leaders. It allows you to make tough decisions and lead your team with clarity and direction.

6. *Reduced stress:* Indecision can lead to anxiety and stress, while being decisive can help alleviate these negative feelings and promote a sense of control and empowerment.

7. *Greater success:* When decisive, you are more likely to achieve your goals and succeed in your endeavors. You can make the necessary decisions to move forward and overcome obstacles.

Ways to develop or improve decisiveness:

1. Practice making decisions regularly, even on small matters, to build your confidence and decision-making skills.

2. Before making a decision, gather all relevant information, weigh the pros and cons of each option, and use your critical thinking skills.

3. Set clear goals and priorities to help guide your decision-making process.

4. With a pre-programmed mind, you can trust your instincts and intuition, which can often lead you in the right direction.
5. Seek advice and input from trusted friends, family members, or mentors to gain different perspectives on the situation.
6. Set deadlines for making decisions to prevent procrastination and overthinking.
7. Take responsibility for your decisions and learn from both successful and unsuccessful outcomes.
8. Practice mindfulness and self-awareness to understand your emotions and biases that may influence your decisions.
9. Break down complex decisions into smaller, more manageable steps to avoid feeling overwhelmed.
10. Reflect on past decisions and their outcomes to identify patterns and areas for improvement in your decision-making process.
11. Just do it. Sometimes, you just need to make an immediate decision. Then, figure out the rest as you go along. It's okay if you make a mistake. Own up to it and redirect your course. As you develop your critical thinking skills, you will find that your decision-making ability becomes increasingly more accurate, and you automatically become more decisive.

Decisiveness is a crucial skill that plays a significant role in various aspects of life, including personal growth, professional success, and effective leadership. Being decisive allows you to make quick and confident decisions, leading to better outcomes and opportunities. It helps reduce procrastination, increase productivity, and ensure timely actions are taken. When decisive, you are often seen as proactive and capable of taking charge in challenging situations, making you a valuable asset in both personal and professional settings. Decisiveness also fosters a sense of self-assurance and confidence, which can positively impact your overall well-being and development. Ultimately, cultivating decisiveness is essential for achieving goals, overcoming obstacles, and seizing opportunities in life.

 Reflect:

1. Have you ever worked with a Complainer? How did you deal with this type of behavior? What were the results? What did you do correctly?

2. What changes will you make as a result of this chapter? What is your desired outcome?

3. What are the challenges involved with a Complainer? How do they affect the work environment? Are they solely with one employee or with more than one? What will you do if the issue is with one employee? What will you do if it is widespread?

4. What are some dangers of a complaining employee? What can you do when faced with this situation? What can you add to the list provided in this chapter?

5. What do you know about patience? How can patience be used effectively in your personal and professional life? Describe a time when you lacked patience in a situation. Describe a time when you displayed patience despite challenging circumstances. Compare and contrast each example. What do you notice?

6. Find ways to program patience into your "preprogram." More information about how to "Reprogram Your Pre-Program"

is found in *Elevate Your Mind to Success, Success Is Ele-MENTAL,* and at www.ABookinTime.net.

7. Describe decisiveness. How is this used effectively as a leader? How can it be used effectively in daily life?

8. Rate your current ability to be decisive in your professional life. Rate your current ability to be decisive in your personal life, such as in your family. What are you doing correctly? How can you improve?

9. What are some benefits of decisiveness? How can this be applied to a situation involving a complaining employee?

10. Research more about patience and decisiveness and practice these valuable skills daily.

CHAPTER 11
The Uncommunicator

Uncommunicative employees are like closed books—their potential remains hidden until they choose to open up and share their knowledge and ideas.

—Jill Fandrich

Uncommunicative employees are reluctant or unwilling to communicate with colleagues or managers. They may be unresponsive to emails, phone calls, or in-person discussions and may even withhold important information or feedback. This can create challenges in a work environment, as effective communication is essential for teamwork, problem-solving, and decision-making. Failure to communicate may lead to misunderstandings, missed deadlines, and a lack of cohesion within the team.

Characteristics of Uncommunicators:

1. Avoid social interactions with colleagues and managers.
2. Rarely contribute to team discussions or meetings.
3. Provide minimal or vague responses when asked for information or updates.
4. Show disinterest in building relationships with coworkers.
5. Often appear withdrawn or distant in the workplace.

6. Do not seek clarification or ask questions when unsure about tasks or instructions.
7. May seem unapproachable or difficult to engage in conversation.
8. Tend to work independently and may resist collaborating with others.
9. Demonstrate a lack of enthusiasm or engagement in work-related activities.
10. Struggle to communicate effectively and may come across as unresponsive or uncooperative.

An uncommunicative employee can significantly impact a leader's ability to effectively manage his team and achieve his goals. The leader may experience frustration and confusion when trying to understand the employee's thoughts and concerns. It can also lead to misunderstandings, missed opportunities, and a lack of clarity in the team's direction. The leader may struggle to provide the necessary support and guidance to the Uncommunicator, which can hinder professional development and overall team performance. An uncommunicative employee can create challenges for a leader in fostering a productive and cohesive work environment.

Uncommunicators can negatively impact their colleagues in several ways. They can create a lack of clarity and understanding within the team, leading to confusion and mistakes. This can also result in increased workloads for other employees who have to pick up the slack or correct errors caused by the lack of communication. Furthermore, Uncommunicators can create a tense or uncomfortable work environment, as their poor communication can lead to feelings of frustration, resentment, and isolation among their colleagues. This can ultimately damage team morale and productivity.

The Uncommunicator's behavior can hinder collaboration and teamwork, as effective communication is essential for successful collaboration and achieving common goals. This can also lead to a breakdown in trust and cooperation among team members. Overall, the negative impact of an uncommunicative employee can ripple through the entire team, affecting morale, productivity, and the atmosphere of the work environment.

Ways a leader can effectively work with Uncommunicators:

1. *Build a relationship*: Take the time to get to know the employee and build a positive rapport. This can help create a foundation of trust and make the employee more willing to communicate. Attempt to discover the source of the poor communication. Is the employee always this way? Or is there a circumstantial reason, such as a trauma or struggle within his family? Does the employee have health concerns? Does the employee have an underlying disability or mental health issue causing challenges in communication? Or perhaps, is the employee extraordinarily shy? By building a relationship with the employee, you will gain insight into the cause of the lack of communication and take steps to develop an action plan for better interactions.

2. *Create a safe environment*: Ensure the employee feels comfortable sharing his thoughts and opinions without fear of judgment or reprisal.

3. *Use different communication methods*: Explore alternative communication methods such as email, written notes, or one-on-one meetings to see if the employee is more comfortable communicating in a different format.

4. *Ask open-ended questions*: Encourage the employee to share thoughts and ideas by asking open-ended questions that require more than a yes or no answer.
5. *Provide feedback:* Offer constructive feedback to the employee on communication skills and encourage improvement in a supportive manner.
6. *Offer training or support*: If the employee lacks communication skills due to a lack of confidence or ability, offer training or support to help with improvement.
7. *Set clear expectations*: Clearly communicate the expectations for communication within the team or organization and provide guidance on how the employee can meet those expectations.
8. *Be patient and understanding*: Some employees may need more time to become comfortable communicating, so be patient as they work to improve.
9. *Reassign tasks*: As the employee takes action to improve communication, consider which tasks may need quiet concentration to accomplish. Perhaps there is a need within your team where this employee would make a good fit. Without bending any rules and making special considerations, consider if there is a current duty this employee could fulfill with his specific demeanor.
10. *Examine the hiring process*: Ensure the Job Description you hire for clearly outlines the position's expectations. Perhaps your hiring team isn't screening candidates enough to select the best-qualified person for the position. Consider making changes in the overall hiring process and candidate selection for future new hires.

Highlighted Character Quality:

Cooperation:

What is cooperation, and how does it fit into leadership? Cooperation is the process of working together toward a common goal or objective. It involves people coming together, sharing resources, knowledge, and skills, and coordinating their efforts to achieve a mutually beneficial outcome. Cooperation can occur in various settings, such as in a workplace, community, or among businesses, and is essential for building relationships, solving problems, and achieving success.

Cooperation is used effectively in leadership by fostering a collaborative and inclusive environment where team members are empowered to contribute their ideas and expertise. Leaders encourage open communication and active listening to build trust and strengthen relationships within the team. This approach allows for pooling resources, skills, and perspectives, leading to more innovative and effective solutions to challenges. Cooperation in leadership promotes a sense of shared responsibility and accountability, ultimately leading to higher levels of productivity and success for an organization.

Benefits of cooperation:

1. *Achieving common goals:* Cooperation allows you to work together toward a common goal, leading to more effective and efficient outcomes.
2. *Division of labor:* By cooperating, you can divide tasks and responsibilities, allowing everyone to focus on their strengths and contribute to the group's overall success.

3. *Innovation and problem-solving*: Collaboration encourages sharing ideas and diverse perspectives, leading to creative solutions and innovative approaches to challenges.
4. *Mutual support*: Cooperative relationships provide the support and encouragement you need to overcome obstacles and achieve success.
5. *Building relationships*: Working together fosters trust and camaraderie among others, leading to stronger relationships and a sense of community.
6. *Resource sharing*: Cooperation allows for the pooling of resources, whether financial, intellectual, or physical, to achieve more than can be done individually.
7. *Personal and professional development*: Collaboration with others can help you learn new skills, gain new perspectives, and grow personally and professionally.
8. *Increased productivity*: When you work together, you can leverage each other's strengths and expertise, increasing productivity and effectiveness.
9. *Improved decision-making*: By bringing together different perspectives and expertise, cooperative groups can make more informed and well-rounded decisions.
10. *Collective impact*: Cooperation enables you to have a larger and more significant impact on your communities, organizations, or industries than you would have individually.

Ways to develop or improve cooperation:

1. *Develop clear communication channels*: Open, transparent communication is essential for cooperation. Establishing clear

communication channels, such as regular team meetings or project management tools, can help facilitate better cooperation among team members.

2. *Set common goals and objectives*: Establishing common goals and objectives helps align team members toward a shared purpose, fostering a sense of unity and cooperation.

3. *Encourage collaboration and teamwork*: Promote collaboration and teamwork by creating opportunities for team members to work together on projects and initiatives. This can be achieved through group projects, team-building exercises, or cross-functional task forces.

4. *Provide training and development opportunities*: Investing in training and development programs can help team members improve their skills and knowledge, making them more effective collaborators and contributors to the team.

5. *Foster a positive work environment*: A positive work environment in which team members feel supported, valued, and respected can contribute to a culture of cooperation and collaboration.

6. *Recognize and reward teamwork*: Acknowledge and reward people who demonstrate exceptional cooperation and teamwork, reinforcing the importance of collaboration within the organization.

7. *Lead by example*: Leaders and managers should model cooperative behavior and encourage teamwork within their own interactions, setting a positive example for others to follow.

8. *Encourage diversity*: Embracing diversity and inclusion within the team can lead to different perspectives and ideas, fostering a culture of cooperation and mutual respect.

9. *Foster trust and respect*: Building trust and respect among team members is crucial for promoting cooperation. This can be achieved through open communication, active listening, and a commitment to understanding and valuing each other's perspectives.

10. *Seek and act on feedback*: Encourage team members to provide feedback on cooperation and teamwork within the organization and take action to address any issues or concerns that arise. This demonstrates a commitment to continuous improvement and a willingness to adapt and change for the better.

Developing more cooperation is important because it enables you to work together to solve complex problems, achieve common goals, and create a more peaceful and prosperous work environment. Cooperation fosters mutual understanding, trust, and respect among participants, leading to more effective and sustainable solutions to challenges. It also promotes economic growth, innovation, and cultural exchange, benefiting society as a whole. By fostering cooperation, you can build stronger relationships, promote stability, and create a better future for future generations.

Highlighted Leadership Skill:

"Emotional Intelligence":

What is emotional intelligence, and how does it fit into leadership? Emotional intelligence refers to the ability to understand and manage your own emotions, as well as to understand and navigate the emotions of others. It involves being aware of your own feelings and being able to express them appropriately, as well as being able to empathize with and understand the emotions of others. Emotional intelligence also includes the ability to regulate and control your emotions in a healthy and constructive manner. It is an important skill for building and maintaining healthy relationships and managing stress and conflict.

Emotional intelligence, or emotional insight, is used effectively in leadership to enhance communication, build trust, and create a positive work environment. Leaders with high emotional insight are able to understand and manage their own emotions, as well as empathize with and influence the emotions of others. They are able to effectively navigate challenging situations, resolve conflicts, and motivate their team members. In addition, leaders with emotional insight are able to make decisions with empathy and consideration for the impact on their team. Emotional insight allows leaders to build strong relationships, inspire and motivate their team, and create a positive and productive work culture.

Benefits of emotional intelligence:

1. *Better interpersonal relationships*: With high emotional insight, you are able to understand and empathize with others, leading to more positive and fulfilling relationships.
2. *Effective communication*: Emotional insight enables you to communicate your thoughts and feelings effectively, leading to fewer misunderstandings and conflicts.
3. *Better decision-making*: With high emotional insight, you are able to manage your emotions and think rationally, leading to better decision-making and problem-solving skills.
4. *Reduced stress and anxiety*: Emotional insight allows you to manage your emotions and cope with stress more effectively, leading to better mental health and well-being.

5. *Increased empathy*: With high emotional insight, you are able to understand and relate to the emotions of others, leading to more compassionate and supportive interactions.
6. *Improved leadership skills*: Emotional insight allows you to understand and motivate others, leading to better leadership and team-building abilities.
7. *Greater self-awareness*: Emotional insight enables you to understand your own emotions and motivations, leading to better self-regulation and personal growth.
8. *Enhanced resilience*: High emotional insight allows you to bounce back from setbacks and adapt to change, leading to greater resilience and perseverance.

Ways to develop or improve emotional intelligence:

1. *Practice empathy*: Try to understand and share the feelings of others by actively listening and putting yourself in their shoes.
2. *Self-awareness*: Reflect on your emotions, thoughts, and behaviors to better understand how they impact you and others.
3. *Manage stress*: Learn to recognize and manage your own stress levels to stay calm and composed in challenging situations.
4. *Develop social skills*: Build strong relationships and effective communication with others to improve your emotional insight.
5. *Practice mindfulness*: Engage in mindfulness techniques such as meditation and deep breathing exercises to stay present and in tune with your emotions.

6. *Seek feedback*: Ask for feedback from others on how you handle emotions and use that information to make improvements.

7. *Improve problem-solving skills*: Learn to analyze and solve problems rationally and thoughtfully rather than reacting impulsively to emotional triggers. Use your *critical thinking* skills to reach conclusions logically rather than emotionally.

8. *Build resilience*: Develop the ability to bounce back from setbacks and failures and adapt to change with a positive attitude.

9. *Cultivate optimism*: Focus on the positive aspects of situations and maintain a hopeful and optimistic outlook.

10. *Seek support*: Surround yourself with emotionally intelligent people who can provide guidance and support in improving your own emotional insight.

Improving emotional insight is important because it helps you to better understand and manage your emotions, as well as the emotions of others. This can lead to improved communication, stronger relationships, and better decision-making. In leadership, it is essential to use critical thinking rather than emotion-based reasoning. However, not everyone can grasp this concept. It is, therefore, vital for you to develop emotional intelligence so you can relate to and better understand others and guide them to logical solutions. It also helps you navigate social situations more effectively and can lead to increased empathy and compassion. Improving your emotional insight can lead to greater personal and professional success.

 Reflect:

1. Have you ever worked with an Uncommunicator? How did you deal with this type of behavior? What were the results? What did you do correctly?

2. What changes will you make as a result of this chapter? What is your desired outcome?

3. What are the challenges involved with an Uncommunicator? How do they affect the work environment? Are they solely with one employee or with more than one? What will you do if the issue is with one employee? What will you do if it is widespread?

4. What are some dangers of an uncommunicative employee? What can you do when faced with this situation? What can you add to the list provided in this chapter?

5. What do you know about cooperation? How can cooperation be used effectively in your professional and personal life? Describe a time when you lacked cooperation in a situation. Describe a time when you exemplified cooperation despite challenging circumstances. Compare and contrast each example. What do you notice?

6. Find ways to program cooperation into your "preprogram." More information about how to "Reprogram Your Pre-Program" is found in *Elevate Your Mind to Success, Success Is Ele-MENTAL*, and at www.ABookinTime.net.

7. Describe emotional intelligence. How is this used effectively as a leader? How can it be used effectively in daily life?

8. Rate your current ability to display emotional control in your professional life. Rate your current ability to control emotions

in your personal life, such as in your family. What are you doing correctly? How can you improve?

9. What are some benefits of emotional insight? How can this be applied to a situation involving an uncommunicative employee?

10. Research more about cooperation and emotional intelligence and practice these valuable skills daily.

CHAPTER 12
The Resistor

A resistant employee is like a tree that refuses to bend in the wind but, in doing so, risks breaking under the pressure.

—Jill Fandrich

Resistant employees are unwilling to change, adapt, or comply with company policies, procedures, or directives. They may be uncooperative, argumentative, or defiant in the workplace, making it difficult for management to implement changes or for the team to work effectively. They oppose change and new ideas, making it difficult for the team to adapt and innovate. Resistant employees can be challenging for leaders to manage and may require additional support and communication to address their concerns and improve their performance.

Characteristics of Resistors:

1. *Refusal to adapt to change*: A resistant employee may resist changes in processes, procedures, or technology, preferring to stick to familiar routines.
2. *Negative attitude*: A resistant employee may have a negative outlook on the organization, its leadership, or colleagues, which can impact team morale and productivity.

3. *Lack of cooperation*: A resistant employee may be unwilling to collaborate with others, making it difficult to work as part of a team.
4. *Reluctance to take on new responsibilities*: A resistant employee may be hesitant to take on new tasks or projects, preferring to stay in their current role or workload.
5. *Disengagement*: A resistant employee may show disinterest in work, leading to lower productivity and subpar performance.
6. *Resistance to feedback*: A resistant employee may be unresponsive to constructive criticism or feedback, making it challenging to improve and grow.
7. *Lack of initiative*: A resistant employee may be unwilling to take initiative or show proactivity, waiting to be told what to do rather than taking ownership of responsibilities.
8. *Avoidance of training and development*: A resistant employee may avoid participating in training or professional development opportunities, hindering the organization's growth and overall success.

Resistant employees can negatively affect leadership in several ways. Their resistance can create a toxic work environment by spreading negativity and undermining the leader's authority. This can lead to decreased morale and productivity among other team members. They may also actively challenge or disobey the leader's instructions, causing disruptions and conflict within the team. This can hinder the leader's ability to effectively manage and guide the team toward achieving organizational goals. Furthermore, the presence of Resistors can also erode the leader's credibility and authority, making it difficult for him to gain the respect and trust of the team. Resistant employees can create significant challenges for leadership and impede their ability to lead and manage the team effectively.

Resistors can negatively affect other employees in several ways. Their negative attitude and behavior can spread to other team members, leading to a decrease in morale and motivation. This can result in a decline in team productivity and overall performance. Resistant employees may also resist change and hinder the progress of new initiatives, creating frustration and tension among their colleagues. Their reluctance to adapt to new processes or strategies can also delay projects and impact the team's overall success. Overall, Resistors can create a toxic work environment and hinder the success and well-being of their coworkers.

Ways a leader can effectively work with Resistors:

1. *Understand the root of the resistance*: Take the time to listen and understand the reasons behind the employee's resistance. It could be due to a lack of understanding, fear of change, or personal issues.
2. *Communicate openly and honestly*: Share your perspective and the reasons behind the changes or expectations. Be transparent and open to feedback to build trust and understanding.
3. *Empower and involve the employee*: Involve the Resistor in decision-making processes and give a sense of ownership and responsibility. This can help with feelings of value and motivation to overcome resistance.
4. *Provide support and resources*: Offer the necessary support, resources, and training to help the employee overcome resistance. This can include mentoring, coaching, or additional training to build skills and confidence.

5. *Set clear expectations and consequences*: Clearly outline the expectations and consequences of continued resistance. This can help the employee understand the impact of this behavior and make a decision to change.
6. *Find common ground*: Identify common goals and values to help the employee see the bigger picture and align the behavior with the team or organization's objectives.
7. *Offer incentives and rewards*: Provide incentives or rewards to motivate the employee to overcome the resistance. These can be in the form of recognition, promotions, or other tangible rewards.
8. *Seek feedback and listen*: Continuously seek feedback from the employee and actively listen to concerns and suggestions. This can help build rapport and trust and find common ground for collaboration.
9. *Seek help from a mediator*: If the resistance persists, consider involving a neutral third party to mediate the situation and help find a resolution that works for both the employee and the leader.
10. *Be patient and persistent*: Overcoming resistance takes time and effort. To help the employee overcome resistance, be patient, persistent, and consistent in your approach.

Highlighted Character Quality:

Empathy:

What is empathy, and how does it fit into leadership? Empathy is the ability to understand and share the feelings and emotions of another person. It involves being able to imagine yourself in someone else's situation and to understand their perspective and experiences. Empathy is an important aspect of emotional insight and is essential for building and maintaining positive relationships with others.

Empathy is used effectively in leadership by allowing leaders to understand and connect with their team members on a personal level. This understanding helps leaders better support their team, communicate effectively, and create a positive work environment. Leaders who show empathy can build trust, motivate their team, and make more informed decisions. Additionally, they can cultivate a more inclusive and supportive culture within their organization, leading to improved collaboration and overall success.

Benefits of empathy:

1. *Improved relationships*: Empathy allows you to understand and connect with others on a deeper level, leading to stronger and more meaningful relationships.
2. *Increased understanding*: Empathy enables you to see things from another person's perspective, helping you to better understand their thoughts, feelings, and experiences.
3. *Conflict resolution*: By showing empathy, you can de-escalate conflicts and find mutually beneficial solutions, fostering cooperation and understanding.
4. *Emotional support*: Empathy allows you to provide comfort and support to others in times of need, showing that you care and are there for them.
5. *Reduced prejudice and discrimination*: Empathy helps you to see the humanity in others, leading to more inclusive

and compassionate attitudes toward people from different backgrounds.

6. *Enhanced communication*: Empathy facilitates better communication by encouraging active listening and validating others' feelings and experiences.
7. *Personal growth*: By practicing empathy, you can develop greater self-awareness, emotional insight, and a more compassionate and caring outlook on life.
8. *Health benefits*: Research has shown that empathy can lead to lower stress levels, improved mental health, and overall well-being for both the giver and receiver of empathy.

Ways to develop or improve empathy:

1. *Active listening*: Pay full attention to the person speaking and try to understand his perspective without interrupting or jumping to conclusions.
2. *Practice perspective-taking*: Put yourself in the other person's shoes and try to understand his thoughts, concerns, and experiences.
3. *Cultivate curiosity*: Ask open-ended questions to learn more about the other person's insights and experiences.
4. *Validation*: Acknowledge and validate the other person's opinions and feelings, even if you don't agree with them.
5. *Practice self-reflection:* Reflecting on your own insights and experiences can help you better understand and relate to others.

6. *Read fiction and watch movies*: Engaging with different stories and characters can help you understand other perspectives and emotions.
7. *Volunteer or work with diverse groups*: Engaging with people from different backgrounds and experiences can help you develop a broader understanding of empathy.
8. *Seek feedback*: Ask for feedback from friends, family, or colleagues on how you can improve your empathy skills.
9. *Practice empathy daily*: Make a conscious effort to practice empathy in daily interactions with others, even in small ways.
10. *Seek out resources*: Many books, workshops, and online resources are available to help you improve your empathy skills. Consider seeking out these resources to develop your empathy further.

Empathy is crucial in leadership because it allows leaders to understand and connect with their team members more deeply. While critical thinking is essential for leadership, leaders can create a positive and supportive work environment by showing empathy, building trust and rapport with their team, and fostering a sense of unity and collaboration. Empathy enables leaders to be more understanding of their team members' needs, concerns, and emotions, which can lead to better decision-making and effective problem-solving. Leaders who demonstrate empathy are more likely to inspire and motivate their team, leading to improved productivity, job satisfaction, and overall success.

Highlighted Leadership Skill:

Empowerment:

What is empowerment, and how does it fit into leadership? Empowerment is the process of gaining the knowledge, skills, and confidence to take control of your own life and make decisions that will positively impact your circumstances. It involves giving people the resources, opportunities, and support needed to assert rights, achieve goals, and fulfill potential. Empowerment can take many forms, including access to education, financial independence, leadership opportunities, and the ability to speak up and advocate for yourself. It also involves creating an environment that promotes equality and respect for everyone.

Empowerment is used effectively in leadership by giving employees the autonomy and authority to make decisions and take ownership of their work. This allows them to feel more engaged and motivated, leading to increased productivity and creativity. Effective empowerment also involves providing the necessary support, resources, and training to ensure employees have the skills and knowledge to succeed. Leaders who empower their employees also foster a culture of trust, collaboration, and innovation, leading to a more successful and sustainable organization. Effectively empowering others results in a more engaged, motivated, and high-performing team.

Benefits of empowerment:

1. *Increased motivation and engagement*: Empowerment gives you a sense of ownership and responsibility, leading to higher levels of motivation and engagement in your work.

2. *Improved decision-making*: Empowerment allows you to make decisions and take action independently, leading to faster and more effective decision-making.

3. *Enhanced creativity and innovation*: When empowered, you feel more comfortable taking risks and thinking outside the box, leading to increased creativity and innovation within the organization.

4. *Higher job satisfaction*: Empowerment gives you a sense of control over your work and allows you to use your skills and abilities to their fullest potential, leading to higher job satisfaction.

5. *Increased productivity*: When empowered, you are more likely to take initiative and be proactive, leading to increased productivity and efficiency.

6. *Better problem-solving*: Empowerment allows you to take ownership of problems and find solutions independently, leading to better problem-solving and a more agile organization.

7. *Improved employee retention*: When empowered, you are more likely to feel valued and appreciated, leading to higher levels of employee retention.

8. *Better customer service*: You are likelier to take initiative and go the extra mile to provide excellent customer service.

9. *Cultivates leadership skills*: Empowerment allows you to develop and showcase your leadership skills, leading to a more dynamic and skilled workforce.

10. *Fosters a positive work culture*: Empowerment creates a culture of trust, collaboration, and accountability, leading to a more positive and supportive work environment.

Ways to develop or improve empowerment skills:

1. *Develop self-awareness*: Understand your strengths, weaknesses, and areas for improvement to build a strong foundation for empowerment.
2. *Set goals*: Define and work toward achieving personal and professional goals to increase confidence and motivation.
3. *Enhance communication skills*: Practice active listening, assertiveness, and effective communication to confidently express your thoughts and ideas.
4. *Build resilience*: Develop the ability to bounce back from setbacks and challenges and maintain a positive mindset.
5. *Seek feedback*: Ask colleagues, friends, and mentors for constructive feedback to gain insights and improve your skills.
6. *Learn to make decisions*: Take ownership of your decisions and learn from both successes and failures.
7. *Develop leadership skills*: Volunteer for opportunities to gain experience and develop your leadership skills. For more information, read the three books making up *The Three-Step Process for Personal and Professional Growth* at www.ABookinTime.net.
8. *Improve problem-solving abilities*: Learn to analyze problems, brainstorm solutions, and take action to address challenges. Reread Chapter 10 on decisiveness and further develop those skills.
9. *Expand your knowledge*: Continuously seek out opportunities to learn and grow, whether through formal education, workshops, or self-study.

10. *Practice self-care*: Take care of your physical, mental, and emotional well-being to maintain a healthy and empowered mindset.

Empowerment is important in leadership because it allows you to take ownership of your work and make decisions that impact your success and the success of the organization. When leaders empower their team members, they foster a sense of trust, autonomy, and accountability, which leads to increased motivation, productivity, and innovation. It also helps to develop and retain talent, as people feel valued and are more likely to be engaged and committed to their work. Empowerment in leadership leads to a more dynamic and collaborative work environment, ultimately driving the organization toward its goals and objectives.

Be aware that empowerment may be used negatively or positively. "Good" empowerment is when you are given the tools, resources, and support needed to make decisions and control your own lives using critical thinking and discernment. It allows you to have a sense of agency and autonomy and to feel confident in your abilities. "Inadequate" empowerment, on the other hand, can involve giving you power and authority without the necessary support or guidance. This can make you feel overwhelmed, stressed, or pressured to make decisions you are not equipped to make. "Bad" empowerment can also involve *manipulating or controlling* you under the guise of giving you power, which ultimately undermines your autonomy and self-esteem. Finally, another form of "false" empowerment involves a culture of people feeling *entitled* and *empowered* to think of themselves as reliant and capable in their own ways *only* rather than relying on God for strength and direction. Ensure that you are aware of the differences in empowerment and use it positively as a valued leadership skill.

 Reflect:

1. Have you ever worked with a Resistor? How did you deal with this type of behavior? What were the results? What did you do correctly?

2. What changes will you make as a result of this chapter? What is your desired outcome?

3. What are the challenges involved with a Resistor? How do they affect the work environment? Are they solely with one employee or with more than one? What will you do if the issue is with one employee? What will you do if it is widespread?

4. What are some dangers of a resistant employee? What can you do when faced with this situation? What can you add to the list provided in this chapter?

5. What do you know about empathy? How can empathy be used effectively in your professional and personal life? Describe a time when you lacked empathy in a situation. Describe a time when you displayed empathy despite challenging circumstances. Compare and contrast each example. What do you notice?

6. Find ways to program empathy into your "preprogram." More information about how to "Reprogram Your Pre-Program" is found in *Elevate Your Mind to Success, Success Is Ele-MENTAL,* and at www.ABookinTime.net.

7. Describe empowerment. How is this used effectively as a leader? How can it be used effectively in daily life?

8. Rate your current ability to utilize empowerment in your professional life. Rate your current ability to empower others

in your personal life, such as in your own family. What are you doing correctly? How can you improve?

9. What are some benefits of empowerment? What are some disadvantages of empowerment? How can this be applied to a situation involving a resistant employee?

10. Research more about empathy and empowerment and practice these valuable skills daily.

CHAPTER 13
The Disorganizer

Disorganized employees can be like a hurricane in the office, creating chaos and leaving a trail of unfinished tasks in their wake.

—Jill Fandrich

Disorganized employees are like a puzzle with missing pieces—they may have potential, but without structure and direction, they struggle to come together effectively.

—Jill Fandrich

Disorganized employees have difficulty managing their time, tasks, and work environment. They may frequently miss deadlines, forget important details, lack accountability, and struggle to keep track of their responsibilities. This can lead to inefficiency, errors, and frustration for employees, their colleagues, and the boss.

Characteristics of Disorganizers:

1. *Lack of time management*: Disorganized employees often struggle to prioritize tasks and manage their time effectively, leading to missed deadlines and incomplete projects.
2. *Messy work environment*: Their desk, computer files, and physical workspace may be cluttered and disorganized, making

it difficult for them to find important documents or information when needed.

3. *Forgetfulness:* They may frequently forget important meetings, appointments, or tasks, which can lead to a lack of reliability and follow-through.

4. *Poor communication*: Disorganized employees may struggle to communicate effectively with colleagues and supervisors, leading to misunderstandings and miscommunications.

5. *Lack of accountability*: They may struggle to take ownership of their work and may shift blame to others when things go wrong.

6. *Difficulty prioritizing*: Disorganizers may have trouble identifying and focusing on the most important tasks, which can lead to a lack of productivity and efficiency.

7. *Procrastination*: They may frequently procrastinate and put off important tasks, leading to poor progress and productivity.

8. *Inconsistent performance*: Their work may be inconsistent and unreliable, leading to a lack of trust and confidence from colleagues and supervisors.

Disorganized employees can negatively affect a leader in several ways. Their lack of organization can lead to missed deadlines, incomplete tasks, and a lack of attention to detail, ultimately impacting the team's overall productivity and performance. Disorganizers may cause frustration and stress for the leader, as they must constantly follow up and micromanage to ensure that work is completed on time and to the required standard. This can also negatively impact the leader's workload and ability to focus on his own tasks and responsibilities. Disorganized employees may also negatively impact team morale and cohesion, as their lack of organization can create a sense of disarray and inefficiency within the team. Disorganizers can significantly strain a leader's time, energy, and ability to manage and lead his team effectively.

Disorganizers can have several negative effects on their coworkers. Their disorganization can lead to missed deadlines and incomplete tasks, putting extra pressure on other team members to pick up the slack. This can lead to resentment and frustration among the team, as well as decreased productivity and morale. Disorganized employees may struggle to communicate effectively or maintain clear and organized workspaces, leading to confusion and inefficiency for their colleagues. They can disrupt the workflow and create a stressful and unproductive work environment for their coworkers.

Ways a leader can work with Disorganizers:

1. *Clearly communicate expectations*: Sit down with the employee and clearly outline what is expected regarding organization and time management. Provide specific examples and ask for input on how to improve.
2. *Offer support and resources*: To help improve organizational skills, provide the employee with resources such as organizational tools, time management apps, or training programs.
3. *Set deadlines and check-ins*: Set clear deadlines for tasks and projects and schedule regular check-ins to ensure the employee is on track and offer any necessary support.
4. *Provide feedback*: Offer constructive feedback on the employee's organizational skills and work habits and encourage improvements.

5. *Delegate tasks*: If the employee struggles to stay organized, consider delegating some of the tasks to other team members with stronger organizational skills. Be sure to reassign appropriate projects to the Disorganizer for his specific skill set to reduce the possibility of decreasing morale. Continue to hold the Disorganizer accountable for his actions and quality of work.

6. *Offer coaching or mentoring*: If appropriate, consider assigning a more organized colleague to mentor or coach the disorganized employee on how to improve organizational skills.

7. *Create a structured work environment*: To help the employee stay on track and focused, provide a structured work environment with clear guidelines and expectations.

8. *Address any underlying issues*: If the employee's disorganization is due to personal or external factors, consider having a conversation to address and support him in addressing these issues.

9. *Monitor progress*: Monitor the employee's progress and provide ongoing support and feedback as he works to improve organizational skills. Include benchmarks for the employee to strive for to ensure progress is being made.

10. *Consider alternative roles*: If the employee continues to struggle with the organization despite support and feedback, consider whether there may be a better fit for him within the organization where his skills can be better utilized.

Highlighted Character Quality:

Orderliness:

What is orderliness, and how does it fit into leadership? Orderliness refers to the quality of being neat, organized, and tidy. It involves maintaining a sense of structure and cleanliness in one's surroundings, as well as being systematic and organized in approaching tasks and responsibilities. An orderly person is often seen as having a disciplined and well-maintained lifestyle.

Orderliness is used effectively in leadership by creating structure and organization within a team or organization. This includes setting clear goals and expectations, establishing efficient processes and procedures, and maintaining a well-structured and well-maintained work environment.

Leaders who prioritize orderliness are able to manage their time and resources effectively, make well-informed decisions, and ensure that team members are working toward the same objectives. By creating a sense of order and stability, leaders can also foster a productive and harmonious work environment, which can lead to increased motivation, morale, and overall performance.

Additionally, orderliness in leadership can help to prevent chaos and confusion, minimize errors and inefficiencies, and promote accountability and responsibility among team members. This ultimately contributes to the success and effectiveness of the team or organization as a whole.

Benefits of orderliness:

1. *Reduced stress and anxiety:* When things are in order, there is less clutter and chaos to deal with, which can help reduce

stress and anxiety. *Elevate Your Mind to Success*, available in retail stores or at www.ABookinTime.net, provides more information on decluttering your mind.

2. *Improved productivity*: Orderliness can lead to improved productivity as it allows for easier access to necessary items and reduces the time spent searching for things.

3. *Better time management*: An organized and orderly environment makes prioritizing tasks and managing time easier.

4. *Enhanced focus and concentration*: An orderly environment can help improve focus and concentration as fewer distractions and disruptions occur.

5. *Improved health and safety*: Orderliness can lead to better hygiene and safety, reducing the risk of accidents and promoting cleanliness.

6. *Positive reputation*: Being orderly can improve your personal and professional reputation, as it demonstrates responsibility and reliability. Also, being organized builds confidence in others toward your capabilities.

7. *Reduced financial waste*: With orderliness, there is less likelihood of misplacing or losing items, which can lead to financial savings.

8. *Improved mental clarity*: An organized environment can lead to improved mental clarity and a sense of control, leading to better decision-making and problem-solving.

9. *Enhanced creativity*: An orderly environment can provide a clear and open space for creativity to thrive, with fewer distractions and more room for inspiration.

10. *Better relationships*: Being orderly can lead to better relationships with others, as it demonstrates respect for shared spaces and consideration for others.

Ways to develop or improve orderliness skills:

1. Create a designated space for everything. Whether it's a place for shoes by the door, a specific drawer for office supplies, or a shelf for books, having a designated spot for each item helps maintain order.
2. Implement a regular cleaning and organizing schedule. Set aside time each week to tidy up and put things back in their place. This will prevent clutter from building up and maintain orderliness.
3. Use storage solutions such as baskets, bins, and shelves to keep items organized and out of the way. This can help reduce clutter and create a more organized space.
4. Label items and containers to make them easy to find and put things away. This can help ensure that items are always returned to their proper place, maintaining order.
5. Develop a system for managing paperwork and documents. Use folders, files, and organizers to keep important papers in order and easily accessible. Label everything properly.
6. Minimize and declutter regularly. Keep only the necessary items that bring joy, and eliminate anything no longer useful or wanted.
7. Set clear expectations and rules for everyone in the household or workplace to follow. This can help maintain order and ensure everyone contributes to a tidy environment.

8. "Reprogram Your Pre-Program." Reprogram your mind by first identifying the root cause and reframing it with the supportive, favorable, and orderly thoughts you want it to contain.

9. Create order within your daily business actions. Have a general pattern for how your day is structured, such as when you read emails, make phone calls, and take breaks. This will maximize your time and better prepare you mentally for how your day may play out. It leaves less up to chance.

Orderliness is essential for various reasons, including creating a sense of structure and organization, promoting efficiency and productivity, and reducing stress and anxiety. It helps you stay focused, prioritize tasks, and manage your time effectively. Orderliness also contributes to a positive and professional image, as well as a clean and safe environment. Maintaining orderliness can lead to a more harmonious and successful personal and professional life.

Highlighted Leadership Skill:

Motivation:

What is motivation, and how does it fit into leadership? Motivation is the driving force that compels you to take action, set and achieve goals, and pursue your desires. It can be influenced by internal factors such as personal values, beliefs, and attitudes, as well as external factors such as rewards, recognition, and encouragement. Motivation is crucial in maintaining productivity and perseverance in the face of challenges.

Motivation is used effectively in leadership by understanding the needs and desires of the team members and providing them with the necessary support and encouragement to achieve their goals. This can be done through setting clear and achievable goals, providing regular feedback and recognition, fostering a positive work environment, and offering opportunities for growth and development. Influential leaders also lead by example, demonstrating a strong work ethic and passion for the work, which can inspire and motivate their team members. Leaders can use various motivational techniques such as rewards, incentives, and team-building activities to engage and motivate their team members. Effective leadership involves understanding what motivates the team and using that knowledge to create a supportive and empowering environment.

Benefits of motivation:

1. *Increased productivity*: You are more likely to set and achieve goals, leading to increased productivity in the workplace.
2. *Improved job satisfaction*: You are often more satisfied with your work and feel a sense of accomplishment, leading to higher levels of job satisfaction. You are also more likely to do what it takes to achieve job satisfaction, which can positively impact your colleagues and employer as well.
3. *Better performance*: Motivation can lead to improved performance, as you are more likely to make an effort to achieve your goals.
4. *Higher levels of engagement*: You are more engaged with your work and are more likely to be proactive and take initiative.
5. *Enhanced creativity and innovation*: You are more likely to think outside the box and devise creative solutions to problems.

6. *Better physical and mental health*: Motivation can improve well-being and reduce stress levels, giving you a sense of purpose and fulfillment.
7. *Increased resilience*: You are better able to bounce back from setbacks and challenges as you are driven to overcome obstacles and achieve your goals.
8. *Positive impact on relationships*: You are often more positive and enthusiastic, which can positively impact your relationships with colleagues, friends, and family.
9. *Personal growth and development*: Motivation can lead to personal growth and development as you are more likely to seek new opportunities and challenges.
10. *Overall happiness and fulfillment*: Motivation can lead to a sense of joy and fulfillment as you work toward achieving your goals and aspirations.

Ways to develop or improve motivation:

1. *Set clear goals*: Specific, achievable goals can provide a sense of direction and purpose, which can boost motivation. Expand your thinking to goals you've pushed aside or didn't think were possible. Consider getting creative with your goals and building your desire.
2. *Find your passion*: Engage in activities that you are passionate about, as this can increase your enthusiasm and motivation. What are you most passionate about?
3. *Break tasks into smaller steps*: Breaking down large tasks into smaller, manageable steps can make them feel less overwhelming and more achievable, which can improve motivation. Slowly build up to bigger goals.

4. *Reward yourself*: Set up a system of rewards for completing tasks or reaching goals. This can motivate you and give you a sense of accomplishment. Make it fun.

5. *Surround yourself with motivated people*: Being around others who are motivated and driven can be contagious and help boost your own motivation. Think of five people you find motivating. Make plans to spend more time with them.

6. *Visualize success*: Visualizing yourself in achieving your goals can increase motivation and drive.

7. *Focus on the positive*: Instead of dwelling on failures or setbacks, focus on the positive aspects of your progress and use them as motivation to keep going. Name three positive aspects.

8. *Take breaks*: Regular breaks and giving yourself time to rest and recharge can help prevent burnout and increase motivation. When was the last time you took a detox bath? How did you feel after?

9. *Practice self-care*: Taking care of your physical and mental well-being can help improve motivation and energy levels. Natural self-care methods can be found on the Natural Pharmacist tab at www.ABookinTime.net.

10. *Seek support*: Surround yourself with supportive and encouraging people who can help boost your motivation and keep you accountable.

Motivation is important because it drives you to achieve your goals and overcome obstacles. It provides the energy, determination, and focus needed to pursue success and helps you stay committed and persistent in your efforts. Motivation also plays a crucial role in increasing productivity, improving performance, and promoting personal growth. It can lead to a positive mindset, increased self-confidence, and a sense of fulfillment, ultimately contributing to overall well-being and success in various aspects of life.

 Reflect:

1. Have you ever worked with a Disorganizer? How did you deal with this type of behavior? What were the results? What did you do correctly?

2. What changes will you make as a result of this chapter? What is your desired outcome?

3. What are the challenges involved with a Disorganizer? How do they affect the work environment? Are they solely with one employee or with more than one? What will you do if the issue is with one employee? What will you do if it is widespread?

4. What are some dangers of a disorganized employee? What can you do when faced with this situation? What can you add to the list provided in this chapter?

5. What do you know about orderliness? How can orderliness be used effectively in your professional and personal life? Describe a time when you lacked order in a situation. Describe a time when you were orderly despite challenging circumstances. Compare and contrast each example. What do you notice?

6. Find ways to program orderliness into your "preprogram." More information about how to "Reprogram Your Pre-Program" is found in *Elevate Your Mind to Success, Success Is Ele-MENTAL*, and at www.ABookinTime.net.

7. Describe motivation. How is this used effectively as a leader? How can it be used effectively in daily life?

8. Rate your current ability to utilize motivation in your professional life. Rate your current ability to motivate others in your personal life, such as in your family. What are you doing correctly? How can you improve?

9. What are some benefits of motivation? How can this be applied to a situation involving a disorganized employee?

10. Research more about orderliness and motivation and practice these valuable skills daily.

CHAPTER 14
The Unproducer

Unproductive employees are like broken tools—they may be present, but they are of no use to anyone.

—Jill Fandrich

Unproductive employees are people who do not effectively contribute to their work, do not complete tasks in a timely manner, or do not meet performance expectations. This can be due to a lack of motivation, skills, drive, or effort. Unproductive employees can negatively impact a company's or team's overall productivity and success.

Characteristics of Unproducers:

1. *Lack of motivation*: Unproductive employees may lack enthusiasm or drive to complete tasks and show little interest in their work.
2. *Poor time management*: They may struggle to prioritize tasks and manage their time effectively, leading to missed deadlines and incomplete projects.
3. *Low energy and engagement*: Unproductive employees may appear disengaged, lethargic, or uninterested in their work, leading to a lack of focus and productivity.

4. *Resistance to feedback and improvement*: They may be unwilling to accept constructive criticism or make changes to improve their performance.
5. *Procrastination*: Unproducers may consistently put off tasks and delay completing assignments, leading to a backlog of work and missed opportunities.
6. *Lack of accountability*: Unproductive employees may avoid taking responsibility for their actions and shift blame onto others.
7. *Poor communication*: They may struggle to communicate effectively with colleagues, leading to misunderstandings and inefficiencies in teamwork.
8. *Negative attitude*: Unproducers may have a negative attitude toward their work, colleagues, and company, which can have a demoralizing effect on the team.
9. *Inconsistent performance*: They may have periods of high productivity followed by extended periods of low productivity, which can lead to unpredictable work output.
10. *Lack of initiative*: Unproductive employees may wait to be told what to do rather than taking the initiative to seek new tasks and opportunities for growth.

Unproductive employees can negatively affect leaders in several ways. They can create a drag on the productivity of the entire team, causing delays and missed deadlines. This can put pressure on leaders to pick up the slack and impact their own performance and stress levels. Unproducers can also create a negative atmosphere in the workplace, leading to decreased morale and motivation among the team. Leaders may have to spend extra time and effort monitoring and managing them, taking away from their ability to focus on other important tasks. Overall, unproductive employees can create a ripple effect that impacts the entire team and puts strain on leaders.

Unproducers can negatively affect other employees in several ways. Their lack of productivity can create additional work for their colleagues, causing resentment and frustration. This can lead to decreased morale and motivation among the team, as other employees may feel that their efforts are not being recognized or appreciated. They may also set a poor example for their colleagues, leading to a decrease in work ethic and performance. This can create a negative work environment and impact the overall success of the team.

Unproductive employees can also hinder the progress of projects and tasks, causing delays and potentially affecting the entire team's success. This can lead to missed deadlines, decreased efficiency, and, ultimately, a negative impact on the company's bottom line. Overall, Unproducers can have a detrimental effect on their colleagues, leading to decreased morale, motivation, and productivity within the team.

Ways a leader can work with Unproducers:

1. *Communicate*: Have an open and honest conversation with the employee to understand why he lacks productivity. Listen to his concerns and provide support and guidance.
2. *Set clear expectations*: Clearly outline the employee's goals and expectations and provide him with the necessary resources and support to meet those expectations.

3. *Provide feedback*: Provide constructive feedback on the employee's performance regularly and work together to identify areas for improvement.

4. *Offer training and development*: Provide opportunities for the employee to enhance his skills and knowledge through training and development programs.

5. *Motivate and inspire*: Encourage the employee to set personal and professional goals and provide him with the motivation and inspiration to achieve those goals.

6. *Hold them accountable*: Set up a system for tracking the employee's progress and hold him accountable for his performance.

7. *Offer support*: Provide support and resources to help the employee overcome any obstacles that may be hindering his productivity.

8. *Seek input*: Ask the employee for input on how he can improve his productivity and work together to develop an improvement plan.

9. *Consider alternative roles*: If the employee is consistently unproductive in his current role, consider reassigning him to a different position that better suits his skills and strengths.

10. *Address any underlying issues*: If the employee's lack of productivity is due to personal or professional issues, work with him to address those issues and provide the necessary support.

Highlighted Character Quality:

Positivity:

What is positivity, and how does it fit into leadership? Positivity is the state or character of being positive, optimistic, and hopeful. It involves focusing on the good aspects of a situation, maintaining an optimistic outlook, and having a constructive and hopeful attitude. Positivity can also refer to the quality of being encouraging, supportive, and uplifting to yourself and others.

Positivity is used effectively in leadership by creating a supportive and encouraging work environment. Leaders who demonstrate positivity are able to inspire and motivate their team members, leading to better morale and higher productivity. Positivity also helps to foster a culture of collaboration and innovation, as team members feel more comfortable sharing their ideas and taking risks. Leaders who maintain a positive attitude are better equipped to handle challenges and setbacks, which can help to maintain a sense of optimism and resilience within the organization. Positivity in leadership can lead to a more engaged and satisfied workforce, ultimately contributing to the organization's success.

Benefits of positivity:

1. *Improved mental and emotional well-being:* Positivity can lead to reduced stress, anxiety, and depression and overall better mental health.
2. *Enhanced physical health:* Research has shown that maintaining a positive outlook can lead to better physical health, including lower blood pressure, reduced risk of heart disease, and improved immune function.

3. *Better relationships*: Positivity can lead to better communication, empathy, and understanding in relationships, leading to stronger connections and more fulfilling interactions with others.
4. *Increased resilience*: A positive mindset can help you better cope with and bounce back from challenges and setbacks, making you more resilient in the face of adversity.
5. *Improved productivity and performance*: Positivity has been linked to increased creativity, motivation, and productivity, which can lead to better performance in both personal and professional endeavors.
6. *Greater overall satisfaction and happiness*: Maintaining a positive outlook can lead to a greater sense of contentment, fulfillment, and overall happiness in life.
7. *Longevity*: Studies have shown that maintaining a positive attitude can lead to a longer life expectancy and better overall health as you age.
8. *Greater optimism and hope for the future*: Positivity can lead to a greater sense of hope and optimism for the future, helping you approach challenges with a can-do attitude.

Ways to develop or improve positivity:

1. *Practice gratitude*: Take time each day to think about the things you are grateful for and write them down if possible. This can help shift your focus to the positive aspects of your life.
2. *Surround yourself with positive people*: Spend time with friends and family who are supportive and upbeat, as their positivity can rub off on you.

3. *Engage in activities that bring you joy*: Whether it's a hobby, exercise, or spending time in nature, engaging in activities that bring you happiness can increase your overall positivity.

4. *Practice mindfulness and meditation*: These practices can help you become more aware of your thoughts and emotions and can lead to a more positive outlook on life.

5. *Set and achieve small goals*: Accomplishing small goals can boost your confidence and overall positivity. Set yourself up for a few good wins before expanding your reach to more challenging goals.

6. *Limit exposure to negativity*: Avoid negative news, social media, and people who bring you down. Instead, focus on uplifting and positive content.

7. *Help others*: Volunteering or helping others in need can bring a sense of fulfillment and positivity.

8. *Take care of your physical health*: Eating well, exercising, staying hydrated, and getting enough sleep can positively impact your overall mood and outlook on life.

9. *Practice positive self-talk*: Be mindful of how you speak to and about yourself, and try to replace negative thoughts with positive affirmations or declarations.

10. *Seek professional help if needed*: If you are struggling with negativity or mental health issues, consider seeking help from a therapist or counselor.

11. *Reprogram Your Pre-Program*: As in *Elevate Your Mind to Success*, reprogram your mind with positive thinking.

A positive attitude is essential for several reasons. It can improve mental and emotional well-being, enhance problem-solving abilities, and increase resilience in the face of challenges.

It can strengthen relationships and improve communication with others. Maintaining a positive attitude can also lead to greater motivation, productivity, and broadscale success in both personal and professional endeavors, leading to a happier and more fulfilling life.

Highlighted Leadership Skill:

Resourcefulness:

What is resourcefulness, and how does it fit into leadership? Resourcefulness is finding quick and clever ways to solve problems or overcome challenges using available resources. It involves being creative, adaptable, and able to think outside the box in order to achieve a desired outcome. This skill is often valued in both personal and professional settings as it can lead to more efficient and effective solutions.

Resourcefulness in leadership is the ability to effectively and efficiently use available resources to achieve goals and solve problems. It involves creative problem-solving, thinking outside the box, and maximizing limited resources. Resourceful leaders are able to adapt to changing circumstances, make quick decisions, and find innovative solutions to challenges. They are able to inspire and motivate their teams to do the same, and they are able to leverage the strengths and skills of their team members to maximize their collective resources. Resourcefulness in leadership allows for more efficient and effective decision-making, problem-solving, and goal achievement.

Benefits of resourcefulness:

1. *Cost savings*: Resourcefulness enables you to find alternative, cost-effective solutions to problems or challenges, thus saving money and resources.
2. *Creativity and innovation*: Resourcefulness encourages thinking outside the box and finding new ways to address issues, leading to a culture of creativity and innovation.
3. *Problem-solving skills*: Being resourceful helps you develop strong problem-solving skills as you learn to find solutions with available resources.
4. *Flexibility*: Resourcefulness fosters flexibility and adaptability as you learn to be versatile and make the most of any situation or resources available.
5. *Self-reliance*: Resourcefulness promotes independence and self-reliance as you learn to rely on your own skills and ingenuity to overcome challenges.
6. *Resilience*: Resourcefulness helps you develop resilience as you learn to bounce back from setbacks and find solutions in difficult situations.
7. *Environmental sustainability*: Resourcefulness promotes the efficient use of resources and reduces waste, contributing to environmental sustainability.
8. *Personal growth*: Being resourceful fosters personal growth and development as you learn to overcome obstacles and become more self-reliant and confident.

Ways to develop or improve resourcefulness:

1. *Cultivate a growth mindset:* Embrace challenges and view failures as opportunities to learn and grow. This mindset will help you approach problems with a positive and proactive attitude.
2. *Expand your knowledge and skills:* Continuously seek to learn new things and acquire new skills that can help you in various situations. This could include taking courses, reading books, or seeking out mentors and experts in different fields.
3. *Foster creativity:* Engage in activities that stimulate your creativity, such as brainstorming, journaling, or participating in creative hobbies. This can help you think outside the box and develop innovative solutions to problems.
4. *Practice problem-solving:* Seek out opportunities to solve problems and challenges in your daily life. This could be as simple as finding a more efficient way to complete a task or as complex as tackling a major project at work.
5. *Network and collaborate:* Build a network of diverse and talented individuals who can offer different perspectives and skills. Collaborating with others can help you access a broader range of resources and ideas.
6. *Embrace flexibility:* Be open to change and adaptable in your approach to solving problems. Pivoting and adjusting your strategy when necessary can help you overcome obstacles more effectively.
7. *Take initiative:* Don't wait for opportunities to come to you—actively seek out ways to contribute and make a difference. This could involve volunteering for new projects, proposing ideas for improvement, or taking on leadership roles.

8. *Reflect and learn from experiences*: Take the time to reflect on your past experiences and learn from both your successes and failures. This can help you to develop a deeper understanding of your strengths and areas for improvement.

9. *Set goals and prioritize*: Identify your most important priorities and set clear, actionable goals to work toward. This can help you focus your efforts and maximize your resources.

10. *Stay positive and resilient*: Maintain a positive attitude and persevere in the face of challenges. Resourcefulness often requires resilience and the ability to bounce back from setbacks.

Resourcefulness is an essential skill that allows you to adapt and thrive in various situations. It enables you to find creative and innovative solutions to problems, make the most of limited resources, and achieve your goals. Resourcefulness also fosters independence, resilience, and self-reliance, empowering you to overcome challenges and take advantage of opportunities. This skill is particularly valuable in professional and personal endeavors, as it can lead to increased efficiency, productivity, and success. Overall, resourcefulness plays a crucial role in helping you navigate through life's complexities and achieve your full potential.

 Reflect:

1. Have you ever worked with an Unproducer? How did you deal with this type of behavior? What were the results? What did you do correctly?

2. What changes will you make as a result of this chapter? What is your desired outcome?

3. What are the challenges involved with an Unproducer? How do they affect the work environment? Are they solely with one employee or with more than one? What will you do if the issue is with one employee? What will you do if it is widespread?

4. What are some dangers of an unproductive employee? What can you do when faced with this situation? What can you add to the list provided in this chapter?

5. What do you know about positivity? How can positivity be used effectively in your professional and personal life? Describe a time when you took a negative approach to a situation. Describe a time when you showed positivity despite challenging circumstances. Compare and contrast each example. What do you notice?

6. Find ways to program positivity into your "preprogram." More information about how to "Reprogram Your Pre-Program" is found in *Elevate Your Mind to Success, Success Is Ele-MENTAL*, and at www.ABookinTime.net.

7. Describe resourcefulness. How is this used effectively as a leader? How can it be used effectively in daily life?

8. Rate your current ability to utilize resources effectively in your professional life. Rate your current ability to be resourceful in your personal life, such as in your family. What are you doing correctly? How can you improve?

9. What are some benefits of resourcefulness? How can this be applied to a situation involving an unproductive employee?

10. Research more about positivity and resourcefulness and practice these valuable skills daily.

CHAPTER 15
The "Entitled"

An entitled employee is like a weed in a garden, choking out the growth and potential of those around him. Uprooting and removing his toxic influence takes diligence, care, and priority.

—Jill Fandrich

An entitled employee believes he deserves special treatment, privileges, or rewards in the workplace without necessarily putting in the effort or meeting the expectations of his role. He may display behaviors such as demanding preferential treatment, expecting promotions or raises without merit, or feeling above certain tasks or responsibilities. Entitled employees can create tension and resentment among their colleagues and may negatively impact the morale and productivity of the workplace.

Characteristics of Entitleds:

1. Believe they deserve special treatment or privileges without putting in the necessary effort or work.
2. Expect promotions, raises, or other rewards without demonstrating exceptional performance or meeting expectations.
3. Often complain about their workload or tasks, feeling they are beneath them.

4. Display a sense of entitlement in their interactions with colleagues and superiors, expecting preferential treatment.
5. May refuse to take on certain tasks or responsibilities they feel are beneath them.
6. Lack accountability for their actions and may blame others for their mistakes.
7. Demonstrate a lack of humility and may boast about their accomplishments or skills.
8. Are resistant to feedback or constructive criticism, feeling they are above reproach.
9. May exhibit a lack of teamwork or collaboration, preferring to work independently.
10. Feel entitled to their salary or benefits and feel they deserve more than what is offered.
11. Have overly sensitive emotions, basing their responses on subjective information rather than objectively.

Entitled employees can negatively affect leaders in various ways. These employees often feel entitled, believing they deserve special treatment or privileges simply because of their position, tenure in the company, or other reasons of their own making, such as generational. This can lead to a lack of respect for authority and a disregard for company policies and procedures. Entitled employees may also resist feedback or constructive criticism, making it difficult for leaders to provide guidance or mentorship. This can hinder the development and growth of the employee, as well as the overall productivity and success of the team.

Entitleds may foster a sense of entitlement among their colleagues, creating a toxic work environment. This can lead to resentment and conflict within the team, undermining morale and collaboration. They can also undermine leaders' authority and effectiveness, creating challenges in managing and motivating the team to achieve organizational goals.

Entitled employees can negatively affect their coworkers in several ways. They may expect special treatment or privileges, creating tension and resentment among their colleagues. Their behavior can also disrupt team dynamics by undermining collaboration and creating a sense of competition. Entitleds may refuse to pitch in on group projects, or they may take credit for others' work, leading to frustration and disengagement among their coworkers. They can create a toxic work environment that hinders productivity and morale.

Ways a leader can effectively work with Entitleds:

1. *Set clear expectations*: Communicate clearly with entitled employees about roles, responsibilities, and expectations for their performance. Ensure they understand what is expected of them and the consequences if they fail to meet those expectations.
2. *Provide feedback*: Regularly provide feedback on Entitleds' performance. Be specific about what they are doing well and where they can improve. Encourage open communication and create a space for them to voice their concerns or opinions.
3. *Set boundaries*: Make it clear that entitlement and special treatment will not be tolerated. Set clear boundaries and enforce them consistently. Hold entitled employees accountable for their actions and clarify that they are expected to follow the same rules as everyone else.

4. *Offer development opportunities*: Provide Entitleds with opportunities for growth and development. Offer training, mentorship, and coaching to help them improve their skills and reach their full potential. Encourage them to take ownership of their own development and career progression.

5. *Lead by example*: Demonstrate the behavior you expect from them by modeling humility, empathy, and a strong work ethic. Show them that entitlement is unacceptable in the workplace and that success is earned through hard work and dedication.

6. *Address entitlement directly*: If entitled behavior persists, address it directly with the employee. Provide specific examples of their entitlement and its impact on the team or organization. Offer support and guidance on changing their behavior and improving their performance.

7. *Seek input from others*: If dealing with entitled employees becomes challenging, seek input from other team members, colleagues, or HR professionals. Get a different perspective on the situation and get advice on effectively managing them.

8. *Celebrate successes*: Recognize and celebrate Entitleds' achievements when they demonstrate positive behavior and meet or exceed expectations. Acknowledge their efforts and contributions to the team and provide positive reinforcement to encourage continued growth and improvement.

Highlighted Character Quality:

Humility:

What is humility, and how does it fit into leadership? Humility is the quality of being humble, modest, and unpretentious. It involves having a realistic view of yourself and acknowledging your limitations and imperfections. Humility also involves a willingness to learn from others, admit when you are wrong, and show respect and kindness toward others. It is often considered a virtue and a key component of good character and moral behavior.

Humility is essential for effective leadership as it allows leaders to listen to and learn from others, admit when they are wrong, and give credit to their team members. Humble leaders are able to put the needs and goals of the team above their own ego and are open to feedback and collaboration. This can help to build trust and respect among team members and create a more positive and productive work environment. Humility allows leaders to continuously improve and grow, as they are willing to acknowledge their limitations and seek opportunities for self-improvement. It can help leaders build stronger relationships, make better decisions, and inspire others to do their best work.

Benefits of humility:

1. *Improved relationships*: Humility allows you to see others as equals and treat them respectfully, leading to stronger, more positive relationships with friends, family, and colleagues.
2. *Increased self-awareness*: You are more likely to be aware of your strengths and weaknesses, allowing you to continuously learn and grow.
3. *Better decision-making*: Humility helps you approach situations with an open mind and consider different perspectives, leading to more thoughtful and well-informed decisions.
4. *Greater empathy and compassion*: You are more likely to be empathetic toward others and show compassion, making you more understanding and supportive in your interactions.

5. *Reduced conflict*: Humility can help diffuse tense situations and prevent conflicts from escalating, as you are more willing to listen, compromise, and find common ground.
6. *Increased resilience*: You are better equipped to handle setbacks and challenges, as you are more likely to seek help, learn from your mistakes, and persevere in the face of adversity.
7. *Personal growth*: Humility allows you to acknowledge your own limitations and seek feedback and guidance from others, leading to personal growth and development.

Ways to develop or improve humility:

1. *Practice gratitude*: Cultivate a mindset of thankfulness for everything you have and the people in your life. Recognize that you wouldn't be where you are without the support and contributions of others.
2. *Seek feedback*: Be open to constructive criticism and feedback from others. Use it as an opportunity for growth and self-improvement. This is valuable information to receive.
3. *Listen actively*: Practice listening to others without interrupting or jumping to conclusions. Show genuine interest in other people's perspectives and experiences.
4. *Practice empathy*: Put yourself in other people's shoes and try to understand their feelings, perspectives, and experiences. This will help you develop a greater sense of compassion and humility toward others.
5. *Admit mistakes*: Acknowledge when you've made a mistake and take responsibility for your actions. Apologize sincerely and make amends if necessary.

6. *Serve others*: Volunteer your time and resources to help those in need. This will help you develop a sense of humility and gratitude for what you have and for others.

7. *Reflect on your values*: Reflect on your core values and beliefs. Consider how they align with humility and how you can incorporate them into your daily life.

8. *Practice mindfulness*: Stay present in the moment and be aware of your thoughts, ideas, and actions. This will help you stay grounded and connected to your values.

9. *Learn from others*: Surround yourself with humble people and learn from their example. Observe how they interact with others and handle challenging situations with grace.

10. *Cultivate a growth mindset*: Embrace challenges and setbacks as opportunities for growth and learning. Stay open to new experiences and perspectives, and be willing to adapt and change as needed.

Humility is essential for effective leadership because it allows leaders to acknowledge their own limitations, seek input and feedback from others, and admit when they are wrong. Humble leaders are more open to learning and growth, which can lead to better decision-making and a more inclusive and collaborative work environment. It helps leaders build trust and credibility with their teams, as they are seen as approachable and willing to listen to others. Humility is a key trait for successful leadership as it promotes self-awareness, empathy, openness to new ideas, and a focus on serving others rather than seeking personal recognition.

Highlighted Leadership Skill:

Critical Thinking:

What is critical thinking, and how does it fit into leadership? Critical thinking is a process of analyzing, evaluating, and interpreting information in order to form a well-reasoned judgment or decision. It involves actively and skillfully conceptualizing, applying, analyzing, synthesizing, and evaluating information gathered from observation, experience, reasoning, or communication. Critical thinking helps you think logically, make informed decisions, solve problems, and engage in rational discourse. It is a valuable skill that can be applied in various aspects of life, including academics, work, and everyday information and decisions.

Critical thinking is a key component of effective leadership as it involves analyzing and evaluating information, solving problems, making sound decisions, and thinking creatively. Leaders who apply critical thinking skills are able to assess situations *objectively*, consider multiple perspectives, and develop innovative solutions to complex issues. By using it in their decision-making processes, leaders can make well-informed choices that benefit their organizations and colleagues. Additionally, critical thinking helps leaders navigate uncertainty and ambiguity, adapt to changing circumstances, and anticipate future challenges. Critical thinking is essential for effective leadership, enabling leaders to make informed decisions, solve problems, and drive positive organizational change.

Benefits of critical thinking:

1. *Enhanced decision-making*: Critical thinking allows you to analyze information, evaluate different perspectives, and make well-informed decisions.
2. *Improved problem-solving skills*: Critical thinking helps you identify and address problems effectively by examining evidence, considering alternative solutions, and evaluating potential outcomes using unbiased information.
3. *Increased creativity*: Critical thinking encourages you to think outside the box, explore new ideas, and consider innovative solutions to complex problems.
4. *Better communication*: Critical thinking enables you to articulate your thoughts clearly, listen actively to others, and engage in meaningful discussions that lead to constructive outcomes.
5. *Enhanced logical reasoning*: Critical thinking helps you identify logical fallacies, evaluate arguments, and draw valid conclusions based on evidence and reasoning.
6. *Greater self-awareness*: Critical thinking fosters self-reflection, self-evaluation, and self-regulation, enabling you to understand your own beliefs, biases, and assumptions.
7. *Improved academic performance*: Critical thinking skills are essential for academic success. They enable students to analyze information, synthesize knowledge, and engage critically with course material, improving their decision-making skills.
8. *Enhanced professional skills*: Critical thinking is a valuable skill in the workplace. It enables you to solve problems,

make decisions, and communicate effectively in a variety of professional settings.

9. *Increased resilience*: Critical thinking helps you navigate complex and challenging situations by examining multiple perspectives, considering alternative solutions, and adapting to changing circumstances.

10. *Improved cognitive functioning*: Critical thinking enhances cognitive abilities such as memory, attention, and problem-solving, leading to improved overall mental functioning and cognitive flexibility.

Ways to develop or improve critical thinking skills:

1. *Practice questioning assumptions*: Challenge your own beliefs and assumptions and seek out evidence to support or refute them. This can help you develop a more balanced and informed perspective on different issues.

2. *Engage in debates and discussions*: Discuss with others with different viewpoints, listen carefully, and critically evaluate their arguments. This can help you develop the ability to think critically about complex issues and consider multiple perspectives.

3. *Read widely*: Expose yourself to various sources and viewpoints, including those you may not agree with. This can help you develop a more comprehensive understanding of different perspectives and strengthen your critical thinking skills.

4. *Analyze and evaluate information*: Practice evaluating the credibility and validity of information sources, such as news articles, research studies, and social media posts. Learn to

identify bias, logical fallacies, and unsupported claims in the information you encounter.

5. *Solve problems*: Engage in problem-solving activities and exercises that require analyzing information, considering different solutions, and making informed decisions. This can help you develop your analytical and decision-making skills, which are essential components of critical thinking.

6. *Seek feedback*: Ask for feedback from others on your critical thinking skills, and be open to constructive criticism. This can help you identify areas for improvement and continue to develop your critical thinking abilities.

7. *Practice mindfulness*: Cultivate mindfulness practices, such as meditation and reflective thinking, to enhance your self-awareness and ability to think critically about your own thoughts and actions. This can help you develop a more reflective and thoughtful approach to problem-solving and decision-making.

8. *Take courses or workshops*: Consider enrolling in courses or workshops that focus on critical thinking skills, such as logic, reasoning, and argumentation. These can provide structured opportunities to practice and develop your critical thinking abilities.

Critical thinking is essential in leadership because it allows leaders to make informed and rational decisions, solve complex problems, analyze and evaluate information, and effectively communicate with others. Leaders can use critical thinking skills to navigate ambiguity, consider various perspectives, anticipate potential consequences, and develop innovative solutions. This ability to think critically enables leaders to adapt to changing circumstances, inspire and motivate their teams, and ultimately drive success and growth within their organizations. More information on critical thinking is found in *Who Connects Your Dots?*, *Medically Speaking, Who Connects Your Dots?*, *Students: Who Connects Your Dots?*, and at www.ABookinTime.net.

 Reflect:

1. Have you ever worked with an "Entitled" employee? How did you deal with this type of behavior? What were the results? What did you do correctly?

2. What changes will you make as a result of this chapter? What is your desired outcome?

3. What are the challenges involved with an "Entitled" employee? How do they affect the work environment? Are they solely with one employee or with more than one? What will you do if the issue is with one employee? What will you do if it is widespread?

4. What are some dangers of an entitled employee? What can you do when faced with this situation? What can you add to the list provided in this chapter?

5. What do you know about humility? How can humility be used effectively in your professional and personal life? Describe a time when you lacked humility in a situation. Describe a time when you displayed humility despite challenging circumstances. Compare and contrast each example. What do you notice?

6. Find ways to program humility into your "preprogram." More information about how to "Reprogram Your Pre-Program" is found in *Elevate Your Mind to Success, Success Is Ele-MENTAL*, and at www.ABookinTime.net.

7. Describe critical thinking. How is this used effectively as a leader? How can it be used effectively in daily life?

8. Rate your current ability to think critically in your professional life. Rate your current ability to think critically in your personal life, such as in your family. What are you doing correctly? How can you improve?

9. What are some benefits of critical thinking? How can this be applied to a situation involving an entitled employee?

10. Research more about humility and critical thinking and practice these valuable skills daily.

CHAPTER 16
Conclusion

Effective leaders don't create followers; they create more leaders. Effective employees don't just follow instructions; they take initiative and strive for excellence.

—Jill Fandrich

Relationships are difficult. Interacting with other people, especially ones you haven't personally selected to be around, can be very challenging. Whether you are a type of leader or an employee, it is imperative to gain skills enough to be an effective and productive asset. Employment opportunities are not only a necessity but also a privilege, and actions should be taken to create the most effective atmosphere conducive to constructive and hopefully even enjoyable team collaboration.

In the book *When Leaders Don't Lead*, we covered various behavior patterns of ineffective "leaders." There are many forms of ineffective leaders, and not all categories are covered in this book, but solutions for most ineffectual leaders can likely be found within the described categories. An incompetent leader can cover an array of ineffective leadership. We heard stories about lost leaders and how they had been hired into extravagant positions. Chapter 1 explored the dangers of hiring someone based on convenience rather than competence. Once the issue is identified, it is vital to consider how to approach and effectively interact with the ineffective leader.

The next five chapters follow suit and present the characteristics of other ineffective leaders, including authoritarian, narcissistic, micromanaging, jealous, manipulative, corrupt, and divisive leaders. The common characteristics are described and seasoned with real-life stories regarding how they look in action as they display their lack of leadership skills in a workplace setting. In each category, suggested methods of approaching and working with this " leadership " style are addressed, with a mixture of what you can control and, more importantly, what you *cannot* control. The book demonstrates areas where your effort to intercept may be effective yet also reveals areas where it may be in your best interest to either complacently accept the situation or follow appropriate steps to extend your resignation in exchange for an exciting new opportunity that awaits you.

Caring for yourself is a priority and should not be taken lightly. Take steps daily to boost your body's immunity naturally—and I stress *naturally*. Your body's own immune system is your *best* defense against disease and illness. When you feel well and are in good health, you perform better in your work and are able to navigate the uncertainties and idiosyncrasies of relationships more effectively. Make self-care and your own personal and professional growth a critical part of your process of relationship improvement training. Ideas, suggestions, and even some remedies are sprinkled throughout the book and at www.ABookintime.net for disease prevention, detoxification, and leadership development.

Leaders are not the only category of people shown in *When Leaders Don't Lead,* who encompass areas needing improvement. Part 2, *When Coworkers Don't "Co-Work",* shares descriptions and characteristics of employees who aren't pulling their own weight within the workforce. Nine chapters are included to share with leaders ideas and strategies for working with employees who lack certain skill sets or who are simply slacking or missing the required character quality to perform effective work production. These chapters include descriptions, characteristics, and ways to work with a certain type of employee, including disengaged, procrastinating, micromanaging, complaining, uncommunicative, resistant, disorganized, unproductive, and entitled.

Whether a leader or an employee, interacting with others is a crucial skill to master. Focusing on relationships and obtaining effective communication skills are important to be successful. No matter what your definition of success may be, communication will be a valuable part of this recipe. Include "improved communication" as a key ingredient in your recipe for success. Along with your communication training, *When Leaders Don't Lead* includes character qualities and leadership skills conveniently located within each chapter, with a total of fifteen of each of them to embed into your mind's thinking. Read, research, study, memorize, and practice these qualities and skills for your continued personal and professional growth. Master them all and make them a part of your daily self-improvement process.

The most challenging part of being effective in whatever role you choose is your ability to get along well with others. As mentioned in the opening line, relationships are difficult. If you seek to master the art of communication and relating to other people, you are well on your way to success in any endeavor you choose. Continue to improve your interactions, and be sure to enjoy the journey and marvel at the unique and interesting people you meet along the way. Learn from each interaction and experience you encounter. After all, people are amazing!

 Reflect:

1. How would you describe the ideal leader? How would you describe the ideal employee? Are you currently the leader or the employee? What do you do correctly?

2. What changes will you make as a result of this book? What is your desired outcome?

3. What challenges are involved with any of the changes? How will you overcome them? How could this affect the work environment? Is the issue solely with one employee or leader, or is it with more than one? What will you do if the issue is with one person? What will you do if the issue is widespread?

4. What are some of the dangers of not making any changes? What are some of the benefits of making changes? How has journaling about the behaviors and techniques applied proven beneficial? How about journaling about quality and leadership skill training?

5. What other character qualities would be beneficial? What other leadership skills or strategies come to mind? How can you incorporate them into your mindset and that of other team members as well?

6. Find ways to program these qualities, skills, and strategies into your "preprogram." More information about how to "Reprogram Your Pre-Program" is found in *Elevate Your Mind to Success*, *Success Is Ele-MENTAL*, and at www.ABookinTime.net.

7. How will you utilize these skills in your personal life?

8. Who will you share this information with? Who will benefit most from it?

9. Apply critical thinking to the information you learned. More about critical thinking is found in *Who Connects Your Dots?*, *Medically Speaking, Who Connects Your Dots?*, and *Students: Who Connects Your Dots?*

10. Practice the skills you learned daily.

Journal
Great thinkers are note-*worthy.*

—Jill Fandrich

Date:

Topic:

What is the identified personality concern? What techniques have I tried?

What is the desired outcome?

What mistakes did I make?

How can I do it differently next time?

What did I do right?

What have I learned from this experience?

Other questions:

Journal

Great thinkers are note*-worthy.*

—Jill Fandrich

Date:

Topic:

What is the identified personality concern? What techniques have I tried?

What is the desired outcome?

What mistakes did I make?

How can I do it differently next time?

What did I do right?

What have I learned from this experience?

Other questions:

Journal

Great thinkers are note*-worthy.*

—Jill Fandrich

Date:

Topic:

What is the identified personality concern? What techniques have I tried?

What is the desired outcome?

What mistakes did I make?

How can I do it differently next time?

What did I do right?

What have I learned from this experience?

Other questions:

Journal

Great thinkers are note-*worthy.*

—Jill Fandrich

Date:

Topic:

What is the identified personality concern? What techniques have I tried?

What is the desired outcome?

What mistakes did I make?

How can I do it differently next time?

What did I do right?

What have I learned from this experience?

Other questions:

Journal

Great thinkers are note-*worthy.*

—Jill Fandrich

Date:

Topic:

What is the identified personality concern? What techniques have I tried?

What is the desired outcome?

What mistakes did I make?

How can I do it differently next time?

What did I do right?

What have I learned from this experience?

Other questions:

Journal
Great thinkers are note-*worthy.*

—Jill Fandrich

Date:

Topic:

What is the identified personality concern? What techniques have I tried?

What is the desired outcome?

What mistakes did I make?

How can I do it differently next time?

What did I do right?

What have I learned from this experience?

Other questions:

Journal
Great thinkers are note-*worthy.*

—Jill Fandrich

Date:

Topic:

What is the identified personality concern? What techniques have I tried?

What is the desired outcome?

What mistakes did I make?

How can I do it differently next time?

What did I do right?

What have I learned from this experience?

Other questions:

www.ingramcontent.com/pod-product-compliance
Lightning Source LLC
LaVergne TN
LVHW091632070526
838199LV00044B/1035